Our Soviet Sister

George St. George

OUR
SOVIET
SISTER

Robert B. Luce, Inc.

Washington—New York

Anyone with any knowledge of history also knows that no great social upheavals are possible without female ferment.

Karl Marx.

Without the fullest involvement of women not only in political life, but the universal productive activity, it is impossible to speak not only about socialism, but about complete and stable democracy.

V. I. Lenin.

Contents

"Mrs. President . . . " the author sharing a joke with Alexandra Ya. Ovchinnikova, the President of the Supreme Soviet of the Yakut Autonomous Soviet Republic, a huge autonomous region of Northern Siberia. The territory of Yakutia is four times as large as Texas, and is incalculably rich in diamonds, gold, oil, timber, furs and hydro-electric resources. Ovchinnikova, a full-blooded Yakut, is an engineer and a doctor of history. Some 55% of all the members of the Supreme Soviet are women. Before the revolution only two Yakut women were known to be literate. Now illiteracy has been completely eliminated and over 50% of all students in the institutes of higher learning of Yakutia are women. The Yakuts, people of Turki origin, are the second largest national minority of Siberia.

1.   Introduction

> *In pain you shall bring*
> *forth children, yet your*
> *desire shall be for your*
> *husband, and he shall*
> *rule over you.*
>
> Genesis 3:16.

God has not been kind to woman.

From the dawn of time, outside of a few obscure matriarchal tribal societies, woman has been relegated to the position of second-class human being. The original reason for this is obvious: as long as brute force was the foremost requisite for physical survival, man had to act as protector and provider for his woman and, in fact, rule over her.

With the appearance of property as a personal power symbol, women became items of wealth—to be fought over, accumulated, held, and traded. So many bulls and cows, so many sheep and camels, so many wives, concubines, and marketable virgins.

As more involved religious traditions were replacing pantheistic idolatry, the subhuman nature of woman was divinely confirmed. The three great religions—Judaism, Christianity, and Islam—were in agreement on that one point. Woman was divinely destined to be ruled over by man; male superiority was axiomatic. For some thirty-five centuries no one dared contest this dogma.

In our Western civilization, dominated by Judeo-Christian tradition, churches held the key to woman's prison. Since

9

God made his original covenant with man, man's position was paramount and unassailable.

The first narrow cracks in the once-solid wall of masculine superiority started to appear only in the middle of the nineteenth century. The industrial revolution, first in England and then throughout Western Europe, introduced machines; and suddenly brute strength ceased to be all important. Using machines, women and children could do man's work at a greatly reduced cost and thus assure larger profits to industrial entrepreneurs. The inhuman exploitation of woman's labor which shocked Marx and Engels during that period was nonetheless the dawn of woman's humanization. In countless families throughout Europe, she became a main provider for her family thus upsetting the roles of the sexes decreed that memorable morning in the Garden of Eden.

The age of man was at its nadir; and the age of woman was dawning.

The process of woman's gradual humanization has not been an easy one. Traditional resistance was enormous. But, brick by brick, the walls of the male superiority edifice started to crumble; and as the twentieth century rolled around, it was becoming more and more evident that woman was destined to play a more important role in life than originally assigned to her by traditional religious doctrine.

The first World War brought on the unprecedented development of industrial technology, and woman found herself face to face with a new danger. With the rise of prosperity, her labor became less important; man was again in position to support his family with his own labor, and could in effect again rule over her—this time, economically.

Woman became the main beneficiary of the consumer society, but also its prime victim. She no longer had to earn her living by the sweat of her brow, and could again retreat into the security of her home and devote her life to her functions of motherhood, child care, and homemaking, while perfecting her skills and attractiveness as man's sex partner.

An anomalous situation was gradually developing in the more prosperous industrialized countries, particularly in the United States and Western Europe. On one hand, never before had woman enjoyed so much comfort and overall physical security. Never before had she been so pampered, glamorized, and indulged. Never before had she had so much money to control and spend. In most countries she had won equal political rights with man and, outside of a few societies still tightly controlled by religious traditions, an equal legal position as a full-fledged citizen. In short she had never had it so good.

On the other hand, with the swift rise of material welfare based on overproduction and waste, she found herself the victim of a cruel paradox. Largely released from the necessity of contributing economically, she was more and more pushed back into an arid gadget-studded *hausfrau* limbo, bearing children, caring for them, looking beautiful, and supplying her consort with the prescribed quota of more or less imaginative sex. And gradually going crazy.

Again paradoxically, the prime victims of this unhappy situation were the women belonging to the higher intellectual and economic strata. While less privileged and endowed women were still in demand on the labor market for simple, less attractive and less lucrative tasks, ambitious, well educated, mentally agile and often talented women had been finding more and more of life's avenues closed to them.

The economic structure of free-enterprise consumer societies, built on controlled unemployment to stimulate labor efficiency, had been progressively restricting the opportunities for professionally-trained women. More and more of the once ambitious, well-educated, and talented girls had to resort to male support as the primary source of livelihood. They were encouraged to consume but not produce, to furnish men's domestic comforts rather than share men's responsibilities in creating them.

A highly competitive dog-eat-dog economic philosophy and practice required the extreme exertion of any person's abilities and resources, including time spent in the competitive struggle. Here man, not occupied with the time-consuming tasks of bearing and raising children, had an obvious advantage.

Not that woman herself had been blameless in the gradual erosion of her economic importance—the prime factor assuring independence. She had permitted herself to be demoralized and debauched by the consumer societies' materialistic excesses. All the publicity media had fanned her urge for acquisition of vulgar social-status eccentricities which she could not possibly acquire without overselling herself in the sex market: few single working women could ever afford new sports cars, jewels, mink coats, or luxurious suburban homes.

The disparity in intensity of sex drive between man and woman had always been a powerful weapon for woman: she could turn masculine sex hunger to her advantage even in the most primitive male-dominated societies. But if sex has been woman's powerful ally, it had one glaring drawback: sex appeal is a perishable commodity, certainly not a dependable basis for lasting emotional and economic security.

In recent years the importance of sex has been relentlessly stressed in many Western societies, but this could not fool intelligent woman forever—the price she had to pay for being a glittering sex symbol was much too high in terms of self-respect and dignity.

The woman's liberation movement which has spontaneously flared up in all Western industrial countries, and particularly in the United States, is a significant and important sociological phenomenon. It is by no means as passing a fad as some people seem to think, and even less the subject for music-hall jokes. Today few intelligent people—of either sex —would deny that the exclusion of a considerable segment of the population from creative economic life robs the world of an enormous reservoir of human energy and human talent which can and must be utilized for the general welfare of mankind.

The question facing our world today is not whether woman's liberation should be achieved, for it *will* be achieved in any event, but what are the best and most effective ways of achieving it.

This is why the experience of Soviet woman in this area should be of interest to all intelligent women, and all men interested in bettering our admittedly imperfect world.

On November 28, 1917, the principle of a complete economic, legal, political, cultural, sexual, and even biological equality of the sexes was proclaimed in the vast country covering one-sixth of the earth's surface and peopled by some hundred and thirty different nationalities and ethnic groups with scores of different cultural and religious traditions. The cultural and religious traditions historically supporting the inferior position of woman were outlawed and made criminally punishable. Never before had this problem been attacked on such a broad front and with such fierce determination to solve it once and for all.

The multiracial and multicultural quality of this great experiment gives it a particular significance. It was not merely a Russian or a Soviet phenomenon, but was designed to be applicable to human society in general: an attempt to bring woman out of the kitchens and nurseries into a new era of history by granting her the obvious rights of full humanness, and to force her to assume the full responsibilities inherent in her new position of first-class human being.

Over fifty years have passed since that day, and a great

deal of water and blood have flowed under the bridges of history. Changes and modification have been introduced into the original sweeping design, to fit changing conditions; but the basic principle of woman's equality in all areas of human endeavor have remained substantially unchanged, both in law and in fact.

The true story of Soviet woman is surprisingly little known outside the Soviet Union, and not really known within it because all analytical history there has been colored with political preconception, as is all history throughout the world. There are more conflicting views about this subject than perhaps about any other aspect of the Soviet experiment to redesign human relationships. While some contemporary observers wax ecstatic about the giant achievements of Soviet woman, others are inclined to be almost shocked at how little has been achieved except, they say, in callous exploitation of woman-power without gains scored for woman's personal well-being.

The truth, as always, lies somewhere in between. It is true that twice during the last fifty years the U.S.S.R. has been rebuilt primarily with woman's labor; and once, after the last war, repopulated by her during the remarkable Operation Birthrate. Behind these hard trials, there has been a steady growth of a new kind of independence and dignity of Soviet woman as a human being and a valuable member of her society.

All honest feminists can take heart in Soviet woman's story. But they should realize that many revolutionary concepts of militant feminism have not stood the acid test of time and practical application. Soviet woman has achieved a great deal, but she still has a great deal to achieve; her path has been neither easy nor smooth. In fact, few women in the capitalist world would trade places with their Soviet sisters. But they all can derive a valuable lesson from Soviet woman's experience.

This experience is particularly interesting if we realize

that the world is in a seam of history, with the sewing machine of time tac-tac-tacking as it tries to connect one patch of history to another which is to follow. Astrologers call this the Aquarian Age; economists, sociologists, and politicians have more mundane names, but it well may be the Age of Woman, in her new role as man's constructive and fully responsible helpmate.

It is not the purpose of this book to predict the future. Prophets, often without honor, today are reduced to handicapping horse races. But one thing is certain: whatever the future holds for the human race, woman's role will increase with time in all areas.

In this may lie a substantial hope for humanity's survival. Woman has much to contribute to its welfare, and more importantly, to its peaceful stability—so sadly lacking in the tragic fabric of recent history. After all, woman is biologically and emotionally more dedicated to producing and protecting life than to destroying it.

More than half a century ago, Soviet woman was given a unique opportunity to play a dramatic and difficult part in the construction of a new human society. Her achievements and omissions in this great historical drama are the subject of this work.

Alexandra Kollontai with emancipated women of Central Asia. The women are drinking wine—a symbolic defiance of the Koran dicta. Kollontai, one of Lenin's closest associates, was the first Soviet ambassador to Sweden. (Moscow, circa 1924)

Nadezhda Krupskaya (Lenin's widow) with delegates of the All-Union Congress of Young Women. (Moscow, 1935)

2. Soviet Woman—the First Steps

To understand the position of Soviet woman today, it is necessary to go back to the misty night of November 7, 1917, in Petrograd. Once known as St. Petersburg, the city was renamed in this Russian way in 1914, after the outbreak of World War I.

This was the night of the Bolshevik armed rebellion which became famous as the Great October Revolution. Yes, the date is correct. In Russia the old Julian calendar was still in use then; and in 1918, it was thirteen days behind the more universally-used Gregorian calendar. The Russian date was October 25.

At about 2:30 A.M. on the morning of November 8, the light cruiser *Avrora*, moored in the Neva River, fired a single blank shot out of its fore gun: "the shot heard around the world." It was a prearranged signal which sent waves of armed soldiers and factory workers in a screaming onslaught on the Winter Palace, the seat of the provisional government of Alexander Kerensky, which was guarded by a few military school cadets and soldiers of the Women's Battalion. (Organized after the revolution—an early sign of woman's lib!)

In ten minutes all was over. A new era dawned in Russia, and the world. The first socialist state in history was proclaimed that same night.

So little resistance was encountered during that historic night that throughout the city only five men were killed and fifty-five wounded. Later the Revolution, civil war, and famine were to claim millions of lives and cause untold suffering; but the birth of the new era was practically painless.

17

The new Soviet government—i.e. the government of the Soviets (or councils) of Workers', Peasants', and Soldiers' Deputies—was led by Vladimir Ilyich Ulianov, better known by his revolutionary pseudonym Lenin *, immediately set upon the ambitious task of creating a state based on scientific socialism and completely redesigning all human relationships.

One of the first avowed aims of Lenin was a complete and absolute liberation of women. Throughout his political life there was no point on which he was more vehement. The position of women outraged him; he considered it hateful, horrible, degrading, ugly, and barbaric. Woman, he said, was doubly enslaved everywhere—first by capitalistic exploitation and then by the traditional domestic relationship between the sexes, i.e. by male domination.

Taking his cue from Karl Marx who held that no great social upheaval was possible without a feminine ferment, Lenin went even further. He vowed to leave no stone unturned in the absolute destruction of all traditional man-woman relationships. Not only was woman to be freed from every vestige of sex inequality, but forcefully drawn into the political life and permanent and universal social service on a mass scale. She was to enjoy a position which she had never enjoyed, even in the most advanced democracies. Every single law and custom placing her into a subservient position to man had to be abolished without trace. Her shameful position as a domestic slave was to be wiped out overnight—absolutely and permanently; and she was elevated to full equality with man, with all the rights and duties of complete citizenship.

To appreciate fully the formidable aspect of this task, it is necessary to remember the position which woman had occupied in the Russian empire. This empire was composed of

---

* Meaning in Russian "Lena's", or "Helena's". No explanation of this choice has been found—there was no known Helena in Lenin's life.

people belonging to over a hundred nationalities and ethnic groups with different historical and cultural backgrounds, but with a strong Russian majority (Ukrainians and Belorussians were considered Russians under Tsarist laws).

It was a class society with rigidly delineated distinctions, almost as complex as the traditional Hindu caste structure. There were titled nobles: grand dukes, exalted princes, princes, counts, barons, one herzog and one prinz (both of German extraction as were all the barons). Then came the *dvoriane* (landlords), the *meschiane* (city dwellers) and the *krestiane* (literally Christians, i.e. peasants). There were also classes comparable to medieval guilds—priests, merchants, jurists, etc.—each with several hierarchal subdivisions. It was an archaic and absurd system. While some peasants could be millionaires, there were princes (usually of Tartar origin) tilling the soil.

This was also a theocratic society based on the Greek Orthodox Church, the state religion. All Orthodox priests were paid by the state, and the tsar was head of this all-powerful organization which was, in effect, a branch of the government. All other denominations were discriminated against by law and in fact; Jews and Catholics were practically disfranchised, and Protestants and Moslems fared only somewhat better.

There were tremendous differences in economic stations. While some, but by no means all, of the aristocrats, landlords, merchants, and industrialists possessed enormous wealth (even though often classed in their passports as peasants), the rank-and-file functionaries, small traders, professional people, artisans, and industrial workers were cursed with the lowest standard of living in Europe. Peasants, representing some 80 percent of the population, were living in incredible misery, periodically decimated by famines, sometimes claiming millions of lives. Even though serfs no longer belonged to

their landlords, with all the best land still belonging to the
landed gentry, the Church, or the Crown, they were reduced
to habitual poverty.

What was the position of woman in this archaic and complex society? Obviously it varied greatly according to her social and economic status.

Women belonging to the aristocratic and wealthy classes
were treated more or less as they were in the rest of the European societies, i.e. as sex objects. They were pampered, admired, indulged, "protected," and traded in marriage; they
had little connection with the rest of the people.

Women of the meschiane (middle-class merchants, traders, artisans, and small functionaries) lived in accordance
with a patriarchal code, with girls considered as the property
of their families. Usually uneducated, they were denied practically all personal freedom and particularly freedom of choice
in marriage. This was a stolid, conservative class, looked
down on by the aristocracy and despised by the liberal intelligentsia.

The most emancipated women of all belonged to the intelligentsia—people engaged in liberal professions, artists,
writers, musicians, educators, and some better-educated functionaries. They came mostly from the impoverished landlord
class—those long since detached from any land. This was the
small but enlightened group which had produced a succession
of brilliant writers, composers, scientists, and early revolutionaries, including Lenin (a hereditary landlord on his passport, and the son of a liberal provincial educator). Their
women enjoyed a social equality with men, subject only to the
legal limitations imposed on women in general. Though educational facilities for women were limited, this class produced
many brilliant women who were well educated and took an
active part in life. In 1913, for instance, there were 2,800
women doctors in Russia, representing 10 percent of all doc-

tors practising in the country, a higher percentage than in most European societies of the time. Fully 8 percent of all teachers were women, again a surprisingly high percentage. There were many women writers, poets, artists, and, of course, ballerinas.

The Tsarist administration regarded the intelligentsia with apprehension and suspicion. This class had been responsible for the progressive ideas which had appeared in Russia before the revolution, and for several terroristic acts involving the royal family and high functionaries. The abortive revolution of 1904–5 was for the most part led by university students and young liberal women. Though Lenin consistently referred to himself and his followers as proletarians, the vast majority of early revolutionaries had come from the intelligentsia.

By far the largest segment of the population was the peasants; and the tsars had always considered them the mainstay of their rule. Utterly ignorant, almost totally illiterate, and steeped in religious traditions, they took little interest in any social movement; this was a class apart, with few ambitions and no hopes except an often vain one of surviving each hungry winter. Even though beggar poor, they had a fanatical attachment to the land, their miserable and often unproductive plots, and were traditionally imbued with a sense of property. The early Russian revolutionaries, including Lenin, regarded the peasants as the least promising material for any social change. The history of Russia is replete with peasant riots and uprisings, but they were caused by the incredible misery rather than any true revolutionary ideas.

Peasant women occupied a special position. Never regarded as sex objects, they were first and foremost workers, a very necessary part of every peasant household. Strong backs and sturdy legs were valued much higher than pretty faces; and even though these women were often abused by men, they were generally respected. This was the equality of misery which they shared with their men.

Incredible hardships, the peasant's lot for centuries, served to produce a special breed of both men and women— strong, resilient, and with an extraordinary capacity to bear suffering and misery. They produced soldiers who, often badly led and poorly armed, fought for the tsars with suicidal bravery, and women able to face almost any adversity with fatalistic courage. They were used to the heaviest labor since childhood. These traits served the country well during and since the revolution when women were often called upon to carry the brunt of the several catastrophes which have befallen the republic during its short history.

The industrial proletariat, which Lenin and other Russian Marxist theoreticians considered the most progressive class of all, appeared in the middle of the eighteenth century when the age of industrialization came to Russia. It was composed of impoverished landless peasants who had moved to urban communities in quest of economic survival and had gradually lost their peasant roots. The Russian industrial revolution followed closely the pattern of the one in England which had so outraged Karl Marx and Friedrich Engels, and led them to the scathing condemnation of the inherent barbarism of capitalism. Indeed the early stages of industrial development in Russia were marked by the most ruthless exploitation of the workers; and as machines made brute strength less and less necessary, women and children were hired to work in mills and factories at starvation wages and under the most inhuman conditions. The practice of so-called homework was particularly vicious—women and children were toiling at home doing piecework to help their men survive. The practice often put men out of work and reduced them to utter poverty.

"The involvement of women and children in homework has become a universal practice," wrote Lenin in 1892, citing figures from the official statistical *manual* published in Russia in 1890. "For the sake of illustration let us cite some figures of this exploitation of women in the Moscow province. In the paper industry 10,004 women are employed at home, the children start working at the ages of five to six, at a daily wage of 10 kopecks, and with an annual earning of 17 rubles. The work day among women often reaches eighteen hours. In knitting industries children begin working at six at a daily wage of 10 kopecks and an average yearly income of 22 rubles. The general figures among working women: there are 37,514 such workers in the Moscow province, starting to work at the ages of five to six (in 6 out of 19 industries, involving 32,400 women workers). The average daily earnings—13 kopecks; and the annual income—26 rubles 20 kopecks." (The official gold value of the ruble was 50 cents.)

Despite these frightening figures, Lenin disagreed with Marx who advocated abolishing factory work for women altogether. "Speaking of the changes in people's life brought about by factories, we should admit that the involvement of women and young girls in industry is basically a progressive development." Lenin felt that this was taking the working woman from unproductive domestic slavery, and that it was "incomparably better than the patriarchal immobility of precapitalist social relationships."

Although things had changed greatly since the early days of Russian industrialization, as World War I broke out, the economic level of the Russian industrial worker was the lowest in Europe. And working-class women had to work almost as hard as their men to sustain their pitiful households; because of that, they were never in the degrading position of being mere sex objects, but were valuable and respected members of their family units.

Women of all classes, in old Russia, shared one common fate—the lack of legal rights. All family relationships were handled by the church: the Greek Orthodox church in Slavic regions, and the Moslem theological councils in the Moslem areas. (Islam was the second largest denomination, though representing less than 10 percent of the population.) The smaller denominations lived under their own canon laws. The state had no authority in those areas of human relations, even though, through the church, it exercised it in the daily lives of the people.

More than 80 percent of the entire population belonged to the Greek Orthodox church. (It was unlawful *not* to belong to any denomination in the tsars' Russia.) And this church— as well as all others—denied all legal rights to woman in accordance with the patriarchal Biblical dicta. Man was considered to be divinely ordained to rule over woman, reducing the woman's position to that of man's charge, if not property. Fathers owned their daughters until their marriage, whereupon they passed into their husbands' legal keeping, and had to live the rest of their lives in "love and obedience" to them. They had no separate identity papers: their names were inscribed in their husbands' passports, and only husbands had the right to permit them to have separate identity documents without which no one could live, move, or work in Russia. Husbands had conjugal rights which could be enforced by law. Any runaway wife could be arrested by the police and returned to her husband. Children were also considered to be the father's sole wards. Divorces were available to men on the ground of the wife's infidelity, with the children remaining with the divorced fathers; men's adultery was not even listed among the transgressions in Orthodox canon laws. Even women of aristocratic and wealthy classes had to comply with these rules; Tolstoy describes the situation in *Anna Karenina*. The only way a woman could terminate an unbearable marriage was by killing herself (as Anna did) or by murdering her husband, as many peasant women did, usually by poisoning them.

Since murder (except that of a member of the royal

family) was not a capital crime in Tsarist Russia, women who availed themselves of this "divorce Russian style" were simply sent to Siberia where they were assigned to male exiles as joint householders, i.e. common-law wives. Chekhov describes this practice vividly in *Sakhalin Diaries*. Oddly enough, many of the murderesses found happiness with their new spouses. However, all children born of the unions were considered bastards and this status was marked in their passports.

But if the position of women under Greek Orthodox laws was pitiful, it was incomparably worse in Moslem areas where the particularly grotesque form of the Koranic code, known as *adat* was practised. Moslem women, living in Russia, had no human rights at all. They were mere chattel; sex conveniences and work animals, to be sold and bought by men who had the right to have as many wives as they could afford. Some of these practices violated the basic Russian legal code, but the Tsarist administration took a tolerant view because of the basic loyalty of the Moslem theological authorities to the throne.

Another fate which all women of the Russian empire shared was an almost total lack of education. In 1913, when the last prerevolutionary census was held, 83 percent of all women were found to be illiterate. The vast majority of the remaining 17% were women of the higher classes; among peasant women illiteracy was almost universal. After the Revolution had swept away the higher classes, either physically destroying them or driving them into exile, the percentage of illiterate women remaining was much higher—at least 90 percent, and some estimates go as high as 95 percent.

This was the ponderous structure which the new Soviet government set upon to destroy in order to create "the first socialist state on earth."

Lenin and his government tackled the problem with courage and determination. Immediately upon coming into power, the Soviet government promulgated a number of decrees drastically changing the social structure of the empire—"leaving not a single brick of it unturned," as Lenin expressed it. Overnight all class distinctions, titles, and ranks were abolished. All capital property and means of production were nationalized without any compensation to former owners; all land was to belong to those who tilled it, factories to workers, and buildings to tenants. All property was abolished in fact, with the exception of clothes and personal effects. Wealthy people found themselves paupers overnight; all those who had served the old state—military officers, functionaries, priests, policemen—were out of work and out of privileges. And because the dictatorship of the proletariat was decreed, they were often legally disfranchised altogether. This was to be an instant gigantic leap from an archaic, theocratic, backward agrarian society into scientific socialism of the most radical kind—bordering on communism.

How did the people of Russia react?

There were special conditions which made this whole situation possible. The Revolution came at the tail end of a long, unsuccessful, frustrating war with the Tsarist government acting in such an absurd and erratic manner as to antagonize even those who had traditionally supported it. Even among the aristocracy and wealthy classes the opposition to Tsar Nicholas, and particularly his empress Alexandra, a hysterical woman given to mystical aberrations, was universal. The intelligentsia was lined up solidly against the throne. The middle classes, impoverished by war, inflation, and total disorganization of economic life, had also lost much of their traditional adherence to tsarism. The industrial workers were in open revolt. And the most fatal fact for the Tsar was that great inert masses of peasants were becoming disenchanted with the "divinely ordained Father-Tsar" and his German empress. Fifteen million soldiers, the vast majority of them peasants, were pining for peace. Peace, on any conditions whatsoever.

The first provisional government, composed of members of the liberal intelligentsia, did not appreciate the mood of the country. When it declared its intention of "pursuing the war to a victorious conclusion," its doom was sealed. Meanwhile Lenin and his party took advantage of this matchless historical opportunity. Their mottoes "Immediate Peace" and "All Land to the People" proved to be irresistible to millions of frustrated peasant-soldiers and city workers who eventually supplied the muscle for the practically bloodless overthrow of the provisional government, and the subsequent civil war.

The very first decrees promulgated by the new government secured for it the overwhelming support of the Russian soldiers and workers. "Decree for Peace" and "Decree for Land" were magic phrases of tremendous semantic power in the Russia of those days. The workers in cities, millions of soldiers, and peasants in villages were won to the Revolution by these two magic words—peace and land.

Next came the decree granting the women of Russia a complete liberation from the religious, traditional, and legal limitations imposed upon them for centuries. The last vestige of any inequality between the sexes was declared abolished forever: woman was to have equal rights and equal responsibilities with man in all spheres of life, without exception.

She was to have equal educational, economic, cultural, and political rights and opportunities. The decree dealt a mortal blow to woman's inequality in marriage, virtually destroying the age-old basis of the traditional Russian family.

No new church-performed marriages were to be recognized; all marriages had to be registered in special government offices. Woman did not surrender her legal identity—she could retain her own name if she wished; and to underline the equality of the sexes, her husband could adapt her name as their common name. No conjugal rights were recognized; both parents were equally responsible for the support of their children, or the State assumed this responsibility if they were unwilling or unable to do so. Neither spouse was responsible for the other's support for as long as the other was physically able to work. Divorces were automatically granted upon the unilateral application of either spouse—the other party did not even need to be notified. Any number of marriages and divorces were permitted. Abortions were decreed to be legal and free, with no limitation of number. The very principle of illegitimacy was abolished: all children born to single women had equal rights with those of married parents. This was by far the most radical piece of legislation ever promulgated in this sphere. Of course, it evoked bitter resistance among traditionalists in all classes—often even among women, particularly among those steeped in religious traditions.

There was a sharp reaction to all decrees of the new government. Propertied classes, totally disfranchised by a single decree, were the first to react. Many members of the intelligentsia, including many liberal revolutionaries, were also appalled at the irresponsible and demagogic actions of the new government. Patriots were appalled at the spectre of ending the war in defeat, and even accused Lenin and his party of a sell out to Germany.

But nothing would deter the Soviet government from its course: socialism had to be built. And it was to be built immediately, with the most ruthless destruction of anything remotely connected with the old regime, with nothing and nobody permitted to stand in their way.

Even before the new government could take a proper look at the country which it ruled, it was attacked from all sides by powerful internal and external forces. "White" armies, with the active support of foreign troops belonging to no fewer than fourteen countries, seized all the most productive parts of the former Russian empire, and for the next two years the Soviet state had to fight for its existence on more than a dozen fronts while facing a complete economic collapse in those areas of central Russia which it controlled.

But throughout those terrible years Lenin did not retreat from the basic ideological positions on which the Revolution was based, even when facing dissent among his own party, and even when his proclaimed principles appeared to be utterly unworkable. Among his unshakable principles was the liberation of women.

Was he a feminist?

Undoubtedly his background colored his emotional intolerance to anything even remotely resembling male chauvinism. His father had died early, and he had been brought up by his mother. His older brother was executed for plotting the Tsar's assassination; after this, Lenin formed a close emotional attachment to his two living sisters, an attachment which endured throughout his life. He had a younger brother, but they were never close. It was three women, his mother and two sisters, whom he adored and respected. Later his wife Nadezhda Krupskaya, who followed him into Siberian exile, became his closest friend and collaborator. And throughout his exile in Europe he had been constantly surrounded by women revolutionaries, always brilliant and often handsome. It is small wonder that he had developed a profound respect for women's abilities.

But above all, he was a shrewd practical revolutionary; and he knew that no destruction of the old society was possible without the destruction of the traditional position of woman in it. Unless woman was drawn into participation in life, traditional domesticity would defeat all attempts to build a new order. The celebrated poet of the Revolution V. Mayakovsky expressed this when he called upon his readers "to wring the neck of every canary bird lest it defeats socialism."

But it was one thing to proclaim the principles of woman's liberation, and quite another to implement them. There was a great deal of confusion. Did this mean the abolishment of the family as an institution? Of marriage? Of all conventional man-woman relationships? Did freedom of love mean free love without any regulatory laws?

Again one should remember the chaotic conditions which existed at that juncture. Some fifteen million men had been mobilized into the army since 1914. Many had been killed or taken prisoner, and almost all had stayed away from their wives for years. Now a torrent of these sex-starved males was pouring back into towns and villages where they often found their equally sex-starved wives consorting with other men. Millions of families just ceased to exist as viable units. So what were those men to do? Shack up with the first woman they found or force their free love on any girl they liked?

Some wild excesses followed. Local Soviets were interpreting women's liberation in their own manner. There exists, for instance, the following order issued in Vladimir, a rather large town close to Moscow:

> Upon reaching the age of 18 every maiden becomes state property. Every girl reaching this age and not married must register, at the pain of legal punishment, at the free-love office. She then will have the right to choose for herself any unmarried man between 19 and 50 as her consort. Such selection of wives or husbands will take place once a month. All men between 19 and 50 shall have the right to select for themselves any registered girl even without her consent in the interests of the state. All children of such unions shall become the property of the Republic.

In some of the small and more remote communities even more bizarre occurrences were taking place. There was loose talk about "the general socialization of all women" (?) which was often taken seriously. There were instances of trains with demobilized soldiers halting near villages and soldiers getting out and raping every woman in sight, in the firm belief that this was one of the freedoms won by the Revolution. Needless to say these orgies were causing consternation among women, particularly in rural areas, and this was used by counterrevolutionary agitators, often with success.

All such eccentricities hurt the revolutionary cause, and Lenin was appalled by them. In his interview with Clara Zetkin, a German communist, he expressed his views: "In the sphere of marriage and sexual relations there must be a revolution, in tune with the proletarian one . . . It will involve sexual relations, marriage, family. The filth of the bourgeois marriage, with its difficult termination, with freedom for man and slavery for woman, vile hypocrisy of sexual morality, all this evokes a feeling of deep aversion among all better people . . ."

Then he touched upon the confusion in the sphere of sexual relations: "Of course, thirst requires quenching. But will a normal man under normal conditions drink from a puddle of water in the street? Or even out of a glass of water which has been dirtied by dozens of lips? . . . I am anything but a gloomy ascetic, but this new sexual life practised by our young, and not so young, people often reminds me of a good, old bourgeois bordello. And this has nothing in common with the freedom of love as we communists understand it."

But how did the communists understand it?

Of all Marxist theoreticians only Engels went deeply into the subject, and he admitted that there was no ready Marxist pattern for a final solution of the sex problem. He wrote in *Origins of Family, Private Property and the State,* "What we can predict about the relationship between the sexes after the destruction of the capitalist system, has basically a negative character, and is limited, in most cases, to what we know will be abolished. But what will replace it? This will be determined only upon the appearance of new generations: men who will never be able to buy women for money or other means of power, and women who will never be forced to submit to men for any other reason but true love, nor refuse themselves to men they love for fear of any economic consequences. When such generations appear, they will send to hell all present norms of behavior; they will themselves know how to behave, and will themselves work out a set of attitudes concerning each individual case,—and period."

This, however, was not good enough for the Soviet government which had to resolve the problem practically. Lenin personally had his own view which he expressed in a letter to Inessa Armand, one of his early collaborators, a charming and brilliant woman whom he respected and admired. He insisted that the term "freedom of love" was in itself misleading. According to him the seven freedoms of love important to proletarians were freedom from financial considerations, material worries in general, religious prejudices, parental influences, conformity with society's opinions, middle-class narrow-mindedness; and the shackles of police regulations.

These freedoms had been embodied in early Soviet legislation. Again and again he defended the new laws vehemently as one of the greatest achievements of the new society: "Not one democratic party, not even in the most advanced bourgeois republics, could achieve in scores of years even one-hundredth of what we have achieved in less than one year. We left no stone unturned to destroy the horrible, vile, foul laws based on woman's inequality . . . which still exist in many civilized countries—to the utter shame of the bourgeoisie and capitalism. We have the right to be proud a thousand times of what we have accomplished. But the more we clear the ground from the filthy debris of old laws and establishments, the clearer it becomes that this is only the clearing of the ground for the future building, and not yet the building itself . . . Woman continues to be choked, degraded, debased by small domestic tasks which are monstrously unproductive and which enslave, destroy, exhaust her and numb her mind.*

Since during those early years Lenin was the undisputed spokesman and architect of the Soviet state, his statements are an accurate way to appraise the country's progress. Again and again he called upon women to get out of nurseries and kitchens and take an active part in the building of the new society, in bringing new order into the then reigning chaos: "There can be no social changes unless the greatest masses of women fully participate in them," he declared on November 19, 1918. On February 21, 1920, he urged the election of as many women as possible into the Moscow Soviet. "Our aim is to involve more and more women in the task of running the country. . . . Elect women workers! Both Communists and non-party women—more, more women!"

He was criticized for trying to involve illiterate "household cooks" in politics, but he stood his grounds. "We are not Utopians. We know that cooks cannot start running the country . . . But we demand that the task of running the country be taught immediately to every household cook." ** And then: "Ruling the country woman will learn quickly, and will catch up with man . . . There are more constructive talents among workers and peasant women than we suspect."

Answering Lenin's call, young Bolshevik women organizers went to work.

The part played by these women during the first desperate years of the Revolution deserves to have a book written about it. Mostly young women of the intelligentsia who accepted the Revolution, they worked mightily in order to save the country, and the Revolution. Thousands of them actually fought in the

* V. Lenin. *The Great Beginning.*
** V. Lenin. *Will the Bolsheviks Retain the State Power.*

ranks of the Red Army, and then went into villages in the liberated areas to awaken women to their new responsibilities, and to explain new Soviet laws to them.

General ignorance was their worst enemy. Few women could read and write, and yet Lenin insisted that women be fully represented in all soviets.

The liquidation of illiteracy became the most urgent task. Innumerable makeshift schools and study groups run by women activists or even literate children appeared in cities and villages. This work bore fruit. At first thousands, then tens and hundreds of thousands, and then millions of women started to educate themselves and take part in political life. More and more were being elected to the local soviets, the administrative organs in towns and villages. Some of them were still practically illiterate, but they responded enthusiastically to the government's call to build a new society. Their red kerchiefs became the symbol of their dedication. Vladimir Mayakovsky thus described the new mass movement:

> *"Leaving lathes,*
> *plows and washing tubs,*
> *pulling hair under red kerchiefs,*
> *hundreds of thousands of simple*
> *women*
> *are learning to build, and to rule."*

This mass involvement of women in political life—in government—was one of Lenin's most cherished dreams. Had he not died as early as he did, eventually "household cooks" would have largely ruled Russia, and much subsequent history would have been changed. Unfortunately, those who inherited his power, even though respecting his basic principles, had not shared his extreme enthusiasm in this respect.

The role played by women activists in the early years of the Revolution was titanic. Tens of thousands of them went into every corner of the country preaching the gospel of women's liberation. In rural regions they often met with fierce resistance. Peasants were traditionally conservative, and older men and women often regarded the activities of these "red bitches" with open hostility. Often the women were ambushed, raped, and beaten up. And yet more and more of them went into this all-important work.

If this was a difficult task in the Slavic parts of the country, the conditions were immeasurably worse in the areas dominated by Moslem traditions. The Moslem priests, known as *mullahs,* for centuries had had a stranglehold on all human activities, and they were reluctant to release it. And the weak Soviet state had to tread lightly lest these regions rise up in armed rebellion against it.

Here, the activists had to face daily danger at every turn. *Women in Revolution,* a book published for the fiftieth anniversary of Soviet rule, gave many individual accounts of these women's trials. Seraphima Lubimova wrote:

"Desperately hard was the lot of Eastern woman in pre-revolutionary Russia. In accordance with Moslem tradition, she was not considered human. She was sold and bought for a price known as the *kalym.* Parents often sold their very young daughters into marriage. The husband had an unlimited authority over his wife. He could legally kill her for being unfaithful, starve her, drive her out of his house, torture her, and add any number of wives to the first one.

"Once legally bought, woman had no right to dispose of her life even after her husband's death. Along with other property and cattle, she passed to the eldest male relative who could either keep her for himself, or sell her again.

"All these terrible aspects of slavery continued to exist even after the establishment of Soviet power. It was difficult to eradicate them. I met them when I was sent by the Party to Central Asia in 1923 to work there.

"The economic and cultural backwardness here was indescribable. Among the Turkmens only 0.7 percent of the men were literate; among the better educated Uzbeks only 3 percent. There were no literate women. Modern medicine was unheard of. Sick children were taken to a *mullah* who would sell amulets against all diseases. Women gave birth while squatting over holes in the ground filled with ashes.

"As soon as we became established, women started to appeal to us, secretly of course. The following is a typical case. A woman in the Djetesui district sent us a message: 'My father sold me into marriage when I was five years old. When I was thirteen, my husband claimed me. Soon he married a second, and then a third wife. I ran away and my uncle took me in. Now he has sold me again to another man.' And here is another message: 'My mother wants to sell me to a man I don't like. Is there any law to prevent her from doing it?' Another of our women wrote: 'Djerabai Raisulov sold his eight-year-old daughter Tarsun for three horses, an ox, and a cow. What shall I do?' "

That was no idle question. To interfere with ancient customs was to endanger the very woman one wanted to help.

Selling girls into marriage was an established custom. Girls of four or five were sold in advance, and at eight or nine could be actually forced into sexual intercourse with their husbands, often old men seeking this sort of stimulation for their failing sex appetites. Some of these children were crippled by this practice, others became pregnant and died in labor. The husbands were held blameless for this savagery.

This is how another woman, working in Turkmenia, describes her experience: "We set up a school for local women. One of our first students was murdered by her husband in broad daylight in our school garden. Her husband came to us and said: 'I paid the *kalym* for my wife. I did not permit her to go to school. She came here defying my will. While here she spoke to men, losing respect and forgetting the *adat*. It was my duty to kill her. The Mosque judge will confirm it.' " For some time, even under Soviet power, Mosque judges still exercized their authority; the man went free.

Another activist Lydia Otmar-Stein, who worked in Bukhara, remembers: "One day I was on my way to the market when I met one of my fellow workers and spoke to him. Just a few steps further I was stopped by two mounted men in Soviet militia uniform, arrested, taken to jail and charged . . . with speaking to a man in the street! I told them that I was the president of the women's section of the Party, but that did not help. I had to stay locked up until some Party comrades came over and set me free. When I remember this now, it seems to be a dream. But it wasn't."

She further describes her vain attempts to appeal to local men to help her in her work. "Sometimes when we visited the women's quarters of private houses, men would come over to listen to us. I remember my conversation with a literate young Uzbek. I asked him why he would not teach his young wife to read and write.

" 'What for?' he answered. 'A donkey can't learn anything.'

"When I pointed out that his wife had a head on her shoulders just like he had, he shrugged contemptuously, 'So what? Dogs also have heads.'

"That was the typical attitude towards women in that part of the world, and almost all men were hostile to us."

Elizaveta Popova, working in Kazakhstan, a huge region of virgin steppes, found the conditions there, too, were appalling: "many millions of Kazakh women had no rights at all, and were destined to spend their lives in filth and ignorance. The customs were grotesque and terrifying. Women were given only scraps of food which they prepared for men. They had no idea of even the most rudimentary hygiene.

"A Kazakh village had no medical services, and there was not a single obstetrician for hundreds of kilometers around. Women gave birth while suspended by ropes under their armpits, and in cases of difficult labor a child would be squeezed out by brute force. Children were never washed, but were smeared with goat fat, wrapped in a goat's skin, and put into homemade cradles, covered with goat skins, with holes cut out for the mother's breast. Filth would accumulate inside, but no one seemed to care."

Infant mortality was astronomical. In Kazakhstan it was estimated that only one child in ten lived to the age of one. Despite polygamy and a high birthrate, the Kazakhs were dying out.

Generally, the conditions which existed throughout the Soviet state towards the end of the civil war defied imagination. The country was in shambles, its industry paralyzed, its transport facilities wrecked, its towns and cities in ruins. Worse still, there was another civil war going on between the city populations and the peasants who refused to sell their produce for practically worthless money. Armed parties were sent into the country to forage for food, and they often encountered armed resistance. Barter trade was the only way to obtain anything, and values had become so distorted that a needle could be bartered for a cow, and a grand piano could be exchanged for several pounds of frozen potatoes—if potatoes could be had at all.

To add further to the incredible difficulties of the young Republic, a catastrophic famine, caused by the worst droughts in history, hit the usually productive Volga regions in 1921 and millions of people died of hunger. So desperate had the conditions become that the government had to accept help from its enemies, including the relief program organized by Herbert Hoover.

All foreign experts predicted a swift collapse of Soviet power, and indeed for a while it looked as though the young republic would not be able to survive. Nothing short of a miracle, it seemed, could save it.

Faced with this dire situation, the Communist party at Lenin's initiative, staged a limited strategic retreat from its original rigid positions. The New Economic Policy, known as NEP, was proclaimed in March 1921, permitting some limited private enterprise and trade, and also allowing peasants, after delivering their tax quotas to the state, to sell their surplus produce in the open market. At the same time the financial system was overhauled: new hard currency was introduced, replacing the paper money which had become completely worthless.

Within weeks there was a change. Some consumer goods, previously nonexistent, appeared; and food started to flow into the hungry cities from the villages. There swiftly appeared a new class of "NEP men," small-time wheeler-dealers, who engaged in an orgy of speculation, often reaping huge profits.

However, according to Lenin, the commanding heights of socialism had to remain under state control. All means of production remained in government hands; and a rigid fiscal system was set into operation, with NEP men being periodically shorn of excess profits by tax collectors.

Slowly the country was coming back to normal. But this normal was comparative. The country was still desperately poor by any standards, and life was incredibly hard. Yet, this was an absolutely necessary breathing spell to permit Russia to get back on its feet.

At the same time the government began an intensive program of reconstruction—factories were repaired and put back

into operation, and new industries were built. This required
masses of labor. And this labor was supplied primarily by
women, since there was now a sharp demographic disparity between the sexes, and because most of the young men were
still fighting on many fronts against counterrevolutionary
forces.

Along with this, the government initiated an ambitious
education program—night schools and *rabfaks,* (workers' universities where proletarian origin and literacy were the only requirements). The majority of the students were women who
worked days and studied nights, acquiring skills and professions theretofore considered man's domain. This was the first
instance where Lenin's policy of involving women in the economic life started to pay dividends. Since all able-bodied citizens, man and woman alike, were subject to a universal labor
draft, all women had to work—digging ditches, operating
heavy machinery, repairing factories and plants, and most important, bearing children to prevent a demographic catastrophe.

The appearance of a new moneyed class, the NEP men,
began to affect the moral climate. The comparatively free
economy bred its usual malaise—commercial sex. Once more
there were men who could pay for sex, and there were women
willing to supply it for a price. Once again there were some
consumer goods—even luxury goods—which so often in history proved to be woman's undoing. There again appeared a
class of kept women who usually disguised their activities by
being private secretaries to important functionaries and well-
heeled NEP men.

But in all fairness it should be noted that the vast majority of the women did not succumb to this evil. They were rising to the opportunities brought them by the Revolution. Hundreds of thousands of young girls and young women either
volunteered or were drafted for various industrial projects

where working and living conditions were often incredibly difficult.

At the same time the Party and the Komsomol (Young Communists' League) initiated an intensive new propaganda campaign against loose sex. "It is interesting to note," Friedrich Engels wrote in his *Book of Revelations,* "that in every large revolutionary movement the question of free love always comes to the forefront." It was getting so out of hand in Russia during those years that the Party had to proclaim sex hooliganism a dogmatic political crime. Those accused of it were publicly denounced and condemned in the press and often drummed out of Party organizations and cells. They found themselves pariahs and outcasts in the new puritanical society.

But it was the traditional moral fiber of Russian woman which was more responsible than all the propaganda for preserving both marriage and family, both once attacked as archaic institutions by revolutionary hotheads. Throughout the reconstruction period, the number of marriages kept increasing, and the divorce rate, once catastrophically high, started to fall off. The state had a hand in this. Since all the housing remained under state control even throughout the NEP period, it could be used as an effective weapon. Local soviets and factory and office councils, particularly in cities and in new industrial settlements, allocated available housing. In all new industrial settlements there were long lists of young couples who wished to marry waiting for the first available room large enough to put a bed or even a mattress in, in order to start a joint household. And once any couple got such *pied-à-terre,* it had to stay put. They could quarrel or even divorce, but they would still have to share the same room, and as often as not, the same bed—with very obvious results.

Gradually the birthrate began to rise. Theoretically abortions were permitted and they were free, and the use of contraceptives was by no means forbidden. But there were few medical facilities or contraceptives available, and Russian girls were traditionally completely ignorant of all sex matters. Also, it seemed, a normal young woman preferred motherhood to abortion, feeling that liberation did not depend on abandoning their physiological functions. And even in those desperate years of almost total lack of any material means, mothers and children were singled out by the state for special protection and care, primitive as such care could be. While Lenin was alive, he incessantly demanded that as much as was humanly possible of the meagre resources of the new republic be used to this end.

Lenin died on January 21, 1924, and with him died the first heroic era of the Revolution: a period of incredible hardship and suffering. Millions of people perished and millions more were driven into exile, but the Revolution survived—a fact which even Lenin called a miracle.

Lenin is given credit for setting up the first socialist society in history, built on entirely new principles of human relations, in the country seemingly least prepared for such gigantic experiment. It was also Lenin who guided this society during its first difficult years with messianic and even barbaric determination, often against bitter opposition within his own party. And among his original principles against which he had never deviated was the liberation of women, and their fullest involvement in every sphere of human activity of the new society.

What was woman's role in the survival of the state? It is impossible to determine accurately. But perhaps the strength and participation of her women was the single most important factor which enabled Russia to survive the years when it was torn to pieces by armed hosts of external and internal enemies and by absolutely catastrophic conditions.

3. The Stalin Era

*Article 12: Labor in the U.S.S.R. is
an obligation and a matter of honor
of every citizen able to work in accordance with the principle: He who
does not work, does not eat.*

*Article 122: Woman in the U.S.S.R.
has equal rights with man in all
spheres of economic, state, cultural
and social-political activity. Such
rights are assured by providing her
with guaranteed employment on an
equal basis with man, with equal pay
for equal work, and equal rest, social security, and educational opportunities.*

*Constitution of the Union
of Soviet Socialist Republics.*

The above two articles of the Soviet constitution which,
unlike many other articles, have been faithfully adhered to by
the Soviet government should be pondered carefully by all
serious feminists of the Western world. They should also be
considered by all those who for fifty years have been baffled
by the Soviet state's ability to overcome a steady stream of
crises—including the shattering assault by the most powerful
war machine ever created by man, one supported by the industrial potential of all Europe.

What confounded many politicians and economists was
that the crises were surmounted despite the axiomatic basic
inefficiency of socialist management as it has been practiced

in the Soviet Union since its inception. The centralized inter-locking machinery often resembled the most improbable of the late Rube Goldberg's contraptions, held together by political terror. It had no business working; and according to many anti-Soviet diehards, it never did work.

Some of the leading Soviet personalities frankly admit the extreme difficulties of working within this system, particularly during Joseph Stalin's stranglehold on the country. In his recently published memoirs, A. Yakovlev, the foremost Soviet designer of military aircraft, including a succession of YAK models, describes his conversation with Stalin on the eve of the 1941 war. Yakovlev had been sent to Germany to select and buy some planes and aircraft equipment which Germany, in accordance with the then existing pact with the Soviet Union, had to supply. It should be remembered that those were the days when this material was a life-or-death necessity to the country.

"Comrade Stalin," Yakovlev told his boss, "our system is impossible. We select the equipment and hand the list to our trade mission in Berlin. They study it, and send it to the Ministry of Foreign Trade in Moscow. They again study it there, and send it to the Foreign Currency Department of the State Bank. They again study it; and if they approve it, they send it along with the money to our people in Berlin. This takes months; and by the time the deal is approved, the selected equipment is often already obsolete."

According to Yakovlev, Stalin picked up his telephone and ordered a million gold rubles placed at Yakovlev's disposal for his next trip to Germany. Yakovlev was a brave man to speak this way to the unpredictable Stalin. But he had no choice—Stalin was the only man in the Soviet Union who could cut, effectively and instantly, through the bureaucratic nightmare within which all Soviet specialists and functionaries had to operate.

Obviously such a system could not possibly work. Still there are some historic facts which cannot be denied nor logically explained.

In fifty years an abysmally backward agrarian country with a totally collapsed economy and with an overwhelmingly illiterate population transformed itself into the second most powerful industrial state in the world with remarkably advanced science and technology. And this despite a succession of catastrophic calamities including the shattering 1941–45 war, and over twenty-five years of Stalin's dictatorial rule with its barbaric excesses and mass purges which often paralyzed creative initiative at all levels.

Then how has this impossible miracle been achieved?

Soviet historians credit it to the inherent superiority of the socialist system over all others. They support this with voluminous charts of statistical figures, many of which are habitually dismissed by foreign economists as sheer propaganda. Indeed many Soviet claims are propaganda; but nothing is more dangerous and unwise than to dismiss *all* Soviet claims as propaganda.

Hitler, with an extremely able brain trust of German economic experts at his disposal, paid dearly for this common mistake. Up to the last day in his bunker in burning Berlin, the Fuehrer could never understand—nor could his experts—what made Ivan run when he was supposed to be long since dead.

This question still baffles many foreign economists. What made the Soviet Union survive and emerge victorious despite the bungling and bureaucratic shackles which would have immobilized most long distance runners? Setting the inherent superiority of socialist system aside, what was responsible for the impossible becoming a part of history?

There are several factors.

First of all, it should be remembered that the Russians

are a talented people. With only 10 percent of the population
of the Russian empire participating in any creative activities,
and with 90 percent being utterly illiterate, they had established one of the greatest literary traditions in history, they had
produced some of the most remarkable music, excellent theatre, the best ballet in the world, and many other cultural values
including the most advanced progressive political movement.
Russian scientists in all fields were acclaimed internationally,
long before the advent of the revolution.

It was not for nothing that Stalin, drinking the victory
toast in the Kremlin on May 24, 1945, broke from the accepted tradition and specifically singled out the Russian people as largely responsible for the victory.*

So the Revolution, occuring in a country little prepared
for any social change, also involved a potentially talented people, until then completely divorced from active participation
in life by centuries of political obscurantism and utter ignorance. By breaking this artificially created dam, it had released
a tremendous reservoir of latent human vitality and creative
ability.

And, most important, it swept woman into this flood. It
not only opened all the gates of life for her, but it *forced* her
to pass through them and into a world which until then had
been completely closed to her. She was to supply new vitality
and talent to build a new society, and also an enormous
amount of raw backbreaking labor needed to achieve the goals
set for the country by economic planners.

In the beginning, the thankless dull labor of breaking the
ground with practically bare hands was done primarily by
women. At least some male workers had rudimentary technical training and were familiar with tools, but millions of So-

---

* "I raise this toast to the Russian people, not only because it is
the leading people, but because it possesses clear intelligence,
steady character and patience."

viet girls and women, drawn into work completely unfamiliar to them, had little to offer except strong backs and hands. (It should be remembered that despite all the educational efforts the census of 1925 found some seventy percent of the women still illiterate.)

Many foreign specialists brought to Russia in the 1920's were appalled at the conditions which they found, and many left after their one- or two-year contracts expired, convinced that all Soviet attempts at industrialization were doomed to failure.

When the first Five-Year Plan was drawn and announced in 1928, it was met with open scorn by all foreign experts. This plan emphasized heavy industry to the exclusion of consumer goods already in extremely short supply. The plan called for construction of hundreds of large industrial complexes from scratch—without machinery or tools, without ready raw materials, and without qualified labor. Also without outside help or financial credits.

The civil war left the country with a serious demographic disparity: there were millions more women than men, particularly in the younger age groups. So women had to pitch in— and pitch in they did. Often they were simply drafted and sent into a virgin wilderness, arid in summer and bitterly cold in winter. The hardships which these first builders endured defied imagination. It is small wonder that the expert consensus was that if even half of the original program were fulfilled, it would be tantamount to a miracle.

But this miracle was accomplished, and in four years, not in five. During these four years over 1,500 heavy industrial complexes were built by untrained young workers, most of them girls. By 1932, when the plan was fulfilled, the industrial production of the Soviet Union reached 253 percent of the 1913 level (the last peaceful year under the Tsar). The annual growth of the gross national product (without counting services) during those years was 19.2 percent—an absolutely unique figure in history of industrial nations.

How was this accomplished?

By the titanic effort of the entire people, primarily young enthusiasts, at least half of them girls who had never before held a tool in their hands. Only women historically used to the hardest labor, and never exposed to consumer-society excesses, could generate enthusiasm under the extreme conditions under which they had to work—without proper tools, shelter, and often hungry. There was no question of women burning their brassieres and panties to prove their equality to men, if only because such luxuries did not then exist, and had not even been heard of. An American engineer who worked in Russia during those years remembered two young Russian girls discussing the comparative quality of the *Pravda* and *Izvestia* newsprint as absorbent pads to be worn during menstruation.

Professor N. Amosoff, the internationally famous Soviet heart surgeon and medical cyberneticist, as well as a best-selling writer, thus describes those years. "Young people of my generation had never tasted sugar, and had never worn anything but checkered shirts and canvas shoes. They worked days and studied at night. When I graduated from the medical institute I had a single torn sweater to my name, and no shirt. But there *was* enthusiasm. Those were magnificent years when we saw industrial plants and schools rising all around us, and we felt that there was no limit to our dreams. And there was no limit to the sacrifice we were willing to make to see these dreams come true."

It was during those years that Stalin, supported by foully sycophantic Soviet propaganda, rose to absolute power, and his methods became draconian. The NEP, with its comparative consumer prosperity, was liquidated overnight, tens of thousands of NEP men were stripped of everything they had and packed off in boxcars to dig ditches and cut wood.

Then came the collectivization of agriculture, probably the most controversial of all Stalin's campaigns. But there was nothing original in this measure—it was the part of Lenin's original program: "Small peasant holdings can hold their own against large agricultural enterprises only by the monstrous lowering of their standard of living and by savage backbreaking toil . . . There is *no* salvation for the peasant besides joining the actions of the proletariat . . ." * How Lenin envisioned the proletarianization of the peasantry is not clear, but Stalin went after the task with hammer and tongs. Peasants were in effect ordered to form communal farms.

Only those familiar with the traditional attachment of Russian peasants to their land can appreciate the shock which this order produced. For the first time, Russian *mujiks* understood that the land of which they had been dreaming for centuries and which the Revolution had given them, was to be taken away from them in the sense of property. They resisted violently, attacking and often killing the "collectivizors" sent into the villages.

Stalin's response was savage. He declared war without mercy against the so-called *kulaks* (literally fists, the peasant term for grasping persons). The kulaks, he declared, were to be liquidated as a class. Any peasant householder who had as much as two cows could be classed a kulak, summarily disfranchised, driven out of his land and home, and sent with his family into forced labor camps in the north—to those regions where even young enthusiasts could not be lured to work. Hundreds of thousands, some say millions, of the kulaks were dealt with in this manner, while poorer peasants were ordered to join the *kolkhozes* (collective farms) forthwith.

They responded by sabotage—slaughtering their livestock and destroying their primitive implements before joining

---

* V. Lenin. *Small Holdings in Agriculture.*

the collectives. So fantastic was this orgy of wilful destruction that even Stalin had to call a halt. On March 2, 1930, he published an article under the ludicrous title of "Dizziness from Success" in which he criticized over zealous collectivizors. From that point on, he declared, peasants were to join the kolkhozes on a voluntary basis and those who wished to do so could return to their private plots. Most peasants did, but 21.4 percent of them remained in collective communes, and wisely so it was later proved. The *edinolichniki* (private householders) were facing starvation with their livestock and tools destroyed, and with the government taxing them heavily at every turn.

So acute was this collectivization crisis that, after the last war, speaking to a foreign journalist, Stalin admitted that this was the most dangerous period in entire Soviet history, more critical even than the Nazi invasions.

The success of the first Five-Year Plan brought no respite to Soviet people. The country was resting on a solid industrial base, but that was just the beginning of "the hard years." The second Five Year Plan was initiated in 1933, and was even more ambitious than the first. By this time Stalin's methods had produced sharp opposition within the Party, and Stalin dealt with it drastically. Thousands of Old Bolsheviks, Lenin's collaborators, were arrested, accused of fantastic crimes, and executed. This was the beginning of the reign of terror: people were arrested by thousands and either executed without trial or sent into forced labor camps—a vicious practice which was to become a permanent feature of Stalin's regime. Eventually the number of such slaves would number in the millions— some historians have estimated twenty million, but this might be an exaggeration.

How did the Soviet people react to these excesses?

Professor Amosoff remembers: "Of course we young enthusiasts knew all about those purges, but as long as they hit the Party echelons, simple people did not react. The propaganda pressure was so relentless that many felt that those people were real enemies of the people and had to be dealt with in the harshest manner. We all felt that nothing at all should be permitted to stand on the way during those years—we were mesmerized by the stream of facts and figures showing our successes. The plan had to be fulfilled no matter how many victims this entailed." *

The success of the second Five-Year Plan was almost as dramatic as of the first one. Industrial production reached 5.5 times the 1928 level. By 1937 over 4,500 new industrial complexes had been constructed, many by forced labor, and the annual increase in gross national product for the period reached 17.1 percent. Comparable industrial growth in the United States took forty years, roughly from 1890 to 1929.

Even more striking successes were scored in the field of mass education. By 1935, illiteracy was nonexistent among men and women thirty-five or younger; and primary education had become universal and compulsory, 55 percent of the students were girls.

Stalin is destined to remain one of the most controversial figures in history. His methods were barbaric, his ruthlessness knew no bounds, but his achievements, on an historical level, should not be underestimated, and his popularity among the masses almost reached the point of hysterical adulation. Every propaganda channel had been utilized to create this adulation —and it often took almost sickening forms: Stalin was declared the incomparable genius of all times in all spheres of human activity.

The second Five-Year Plan was also fulfilled largely by the utilization of women's labor, but the women were different now. They were no longer illiterate, and many had ac-

---

* In private conversations with the author.

quired skills and professions which their mothers could not
even dream of. Those were years when femininity was scorned
as a bourgeois weakness: the ideal Soviet woman was glamorized in literature, films and the propaganda media as a muscle-
bound wench digging a canal or driving a tractor and bursting
with socialist enthusiasm. She spent her nights over piles of
books "developing her qualifications."

There was a new purpose in this besides sheer enthusiasm.
The principle of *urovnilovka* (equal distribution of incomes),
was declared to be reactionary, and the old Marxist formula
of "to each according to his needs" was changed to "to each
according to his work." (This last formula was embodied
verbatim in the Soviet constitution and remains there to this
day.) Education had become the key for personal success: specialists drew incomparably higher wages than unskilled workers, and this situation still prevails in Soviet society. Education became almost a craze among young Soviets, particularly
the girls.

By the end of the second plan the level of Soviet industrial production was the highest in Europe, though in terms of
consumer goods the standard of living remained very low. This
enforced personal austerity was compensated for by a sense
of national pride; all new victories on the industrial front were
equated with personal achievements, and this pride was relentlessly fanned by official propaganda. Soviet achievement in
technical areas, such as world records set by Soviet flyers,
evoked popular enthusiasm. At this time practically all out-
standing inventions throughout human history were ascribed
to Russians with the actual facts often twisted out of all sem-
blance to reality.

Stalin has often been accused by orthodox Marxists of
perverting the principles of proletarian internationalism and
substituting for it Soviet chauvinism. Once despised words
such as "patriotism" and "the motherland" became not merely

respectable, but almost sacred. Of course, they meant socialist patriotism and the socialist motherland, but those were meaningless semantic details.

Why did Stalin permit this?

The answer lies in Stalin's being not only a ruthless tyrant, but an extremely shrewd politician. By the mid-1930's it was becoming obvious that sooner or later the Soviet Union would have to face Hitler's Germany; and the purpose of Stalin's government during those years seems to have been to postpone this inevitable showdown for as long as possible, while building up a psychological base, particularly among Soviet youth, for this coming war. A number of measures promulgated during those years pointed towards this goal.

Moral looseness was being ruthlessly eradicated: and slowly, almost imperceptibly, the original liberal laws in the areas of sex, marriage, and family were being tightened. Divorces were made more difficult and very costly. Unregistered marriages, once very common, were frowned upon; and those "practicing love as sport," to use Mayakovsky's definition, were castigated in the press. Unregistered fathers of children born out of wedlock were required to contribute to their children's support, and socialist morality was proclaimed to be a great virtue. The results were immediate. Some 180,000 unregistered marriages were registered the first year after the promulgation of the support law; and the number of divorces decreased drastically. The family was to be again the basis of the socialist society.

The third Five-Year Plan, initiated in March of 1939, remained unfinished because of the war. By this time the collectivization of agriculture was almost complete, over 94 percent of the peasants were working on collective or state farms. Those prewar years demanded particularly hard labor from the Soviet people. The tempo of construction for new war industries was raised drastically, and the government took some draconian measures for the improvement of the country's defense potential. In September of 1939, a universal military draft was put into effect; and in June of 1940, industry was put on a seven-day workweek with workers forbidden to change employment thus becoming, in effect, industrial serfs. New and improved models of various armaments were put into mass production and there was general tightening of discipline in all areas of human activity.

All these measures were known to the Germans; and they decided to strike quickly to finish off the Soviet Union with a single knockout blow. German economic and military experts were convinced that the Soviet multinational state would fall apart—they discarded the Soviet figures for industrial production as sheer propaganda.

The massed German armies struck on June 22, 1941. The history of the war is too well known to describe here. The Nazi armies met some bitter resistance, but quickly overcame it and overran enormous territories where 40 percent of the population lived before the war, and which contained 60 percent of the industrial and 70 percent of the agricultural potential of the country.

Despite these catastrophies, the Soviet Union did not fall apart; and before the year was out the Wehrmacht suffered the first bad defeat in its short but spectacular history. Historians, particularly German ones, are still trying to explain it by such factors as bad weather, intense winter cold, the absence of usable roads, etc.—but the sober fact is that the shattered Soviet industries almost miraculously recovered from the initial knockout blows in a surprisingly short time. By December, during the battle for Moscow, the Soviet troops defending the city could muster air superiority over the attacking Nazis, despite the fact that the Soviet Air Force had been almost totally annihilated five months before.

Only one year after the start of the war, the Soviet Union

could outproduce all combined European industries then under the Nazi control. Much has been written about the heroism of the Soviet troops, but without the support of the Soviet rear nothing could have averted their defeat. It was the remarkable resilience of the Soviet industrial backbone which the German war planners did not take into consideration in their calculations.

Modern industry requires masses of qualified labor in order to deliver the goods. And in Russia this labor was provided, to a large extent, by women—often mere girls, who quickly replaced men in factories, working fourteen to eighteen hours a day often under appalling conditions. Many factories, evacuated to Siberia, started to operate under hastily put up roofs and with no walls to protect the workers from the bitter Siberian cold.

It is enough to remember the nightmarish nine-hundred-day seige of Leningrad during which over 800,000 civilians perished, at least 500,000 of them women and children. And all this time, no day passed without Leningrad factories producing arms and munitions for the troops defending the city.

The heroism of Soviet women during the war is still an unwritten saga; and in the final analysis, this was the factor which spelled the final doom of the terrible Nazi dream.

Women fought in the ranks of the Red Army, particularly in the guerrilla units operating behind the Nazi lines. There were several air regiments "manned" entirely by women flyers. There were thousands of women snipers and machine gunners; and there was no unit in the Red Army without some women in it, mostly in medical and signals services, but also fighting side by side with men. In the diary of Rudnev, the commissar of the celebrated Kavpak guerrilla unit, there is a short, but poignant entry: "Today we evacuated our machine gunner Nina Sozneva. The poor girl has been wounded eight times since the start of the war."

But it was the heroism of Soviet women working in the rear which made the difference, they included girls in their early teens and grandmothers in their sixties. They were no longer illiterate peasant *babas,* but were trained for hard work, inured to suffering and privation, and familiar with the fate the Nazis had in store for them.

The carefully developed feminine ferment in Soviet society proved to be that one hidden factor which misled and bedeviled German military planners throughout the war. These intelligent educated women, blessed with strong moral and physical fiber, proved to be the real Soviet secret weapon, more deadly than the famous Soviet T-34 tanks.

If concrete proof of woman's potential worth as a sustaining backbone of any society was needed, the war years in Russia furnished it.

At the start of the war, Nazi Germany was incalculably better prepared than the Soviet Union, but it had one inherent weakness: the attitude towards women embodied in the Nazis' philosophy. It was based on a medieval German concept of woman's natural role as *hausfrau* and breeder of future soldiers, and all non-German women usable only as household slaves. Only towards the very end of the war did Albert Speer's ministry start drafting German women for war work, but they were uneducated industrially and debauched by many years of the barbaric Nazi philosophy. And there was no question at all of ever using any of them for combat.

It is symbolic indeed that among the Soviet soldiers who stormed and captured the Reich's chancellery, the last Nazi stronghold in shattered Berlin, there was a woman—Major Anna Nikulina.

Since the end of the war, German military historians have been searching for the hidden factor which had escaped the German military planners' attention when they were drafting *Barbarossa,* the blitzkrieg campaign against the Soviet Union.

One of them, Kurt Tippelskirch, blames the Soviet penchant for secrecy for the German failure: "To determine, even approximately, the might of the Soviet Union was almost impossible. There were too many unknown factors which usually can be determined about the mobilization potential of any country's armed forces, and economic facilities sustaining them. In the Soviet Union they represented an impenetrable mystery." *

Then, with purely German precision he calculates the maximum number of men that could possibly be mobilized in the Soviet Union, and the number of men necessary to sustain war industries at the level of productivity necessary for the war. And comes out with a question mark.

And small wonder. Nowhere in all his calculations does he even mention women as a possible source of manpower or, more importantly, of moral power to sustain the men fighting in the front line. The question, "What makes Ivan run?" remains unanswered.

The very simple answer, "Maria," never seems to occur to any of them.

Yet women played an important part in sustaining their men through all the recurring disasters which have befallen Slavic tribes since the dawn of their history. This is not a recent Soviet phenomenon, and many factors have contributed to it. Among the most important were the harsh climate of the eastern European plains and the generally poor soil requiring hard labor to squeeze life out of it—particularly in the northern forest lands which were home of the Slavs for much of their history.

Even during the Revolution and the early struggle for survival of the young Soviet state, women already proved their mettle. Speaking to Klara Zetkin in 1918, Lenin said: "In Petrograd, and here in Moscow, and in all even most remote

---

* K. Tippelskirch. *The History of the Second World War.*

industrial centers, our proletarian women have behaved heroically. Without them we would not have won—at least, we might not have won. What courage have they shown, and what courage they are showing today! Just imagine all the suffering and privations which they have to endure . . . Yes, our women are magnificent . . . They deserve our admiration and love. But then we must admit that even the bourgeois ladies who fought against us have shown more courage than their men."

That was in 1918. By 1941 when Hitler decided to liquidate Bolshevism once and for all and to extend the German *Lebensraum* east to the Urals, new generations of Soviet women had grown up. They were no longer ignorant and browbeaten, but hard and proud of their new position in life. And the Soviet leaders had grown to depend on them.

Some time ago I wrote a letter to Marshal Zhukov, the senior surviving Soviet war leader, asking his opinion about the inexplicably calm behavior of the enigmatic Stalin in the face of the seemingly inevitable disaster which threatened the Soviet Union in the summer of 1941. Zhukov answered that Stalin knew very well that if Hitler attacked the Soviet Union, he would not have enough strength or resources to bring the war to a victorious conclusion.

How could Stalin, or anyone else, know that?

Every available fact and figure pointed in the other direction. Germany had an enormous fully mobilized army with extensive experience in modern warfare. Its equipment was vastly superior, in every department, to that of the Red Army. And this monstrous war machine was backed by the industrial capacity of Germany and all the industrial nations which she had conquered. In 1941 the Nazi empire was annually producing 506,000,000 tons of coal to the Soviet Union's 166,-000,000; 48,500,000 tons of steel to 18,300,000 produced in the Soviet Union; and 126,000 heavy machine tools to 78,400 produced by the Soviet state. These figures, and others just as frightening, were very well known to the Soviet government on the eve of the war.

And within a few days after the start of the war, the disparity became infinitely more lopsided.

Then what was the source of the Soviet government's confidence in Russia's ability to cope with the catastrophe? What made Stalin, on July 6, 1941, when the Red Armies were being cut to pieces and Nazi armored columns rolling deep into the country, declare: "Comrades! Our forces are incalculable. The enemy will have to discover it soon"?

Perhaps an answer can be gleaned from the speech delivered on May 8, 1965 by Leonid Brezhnev for the twentieth anniversary of the Soviet victory:

"Never before had the strength of spirit and the unbending will of our Soviet women, and their boundless loyalty to their country, been demonstrated so dramatically as during the war: both their incredible performance on the labor front and their heroism on the fighting one. The image of our woman with a rifle or a joystick of plane in her hand, the image of a front line medic working under the enemy fire will forever live in our memory as the shining symbol of self-sacrifice and heroism.

"And how much had our women done for victory by their labor in the rear? They labored for themselves, and for all those who had gone to the front. If one could find some gigantic scales and place in one pan the military heroism of our soldiers, and in the other the labor heroism of our women, the scales would have balanced . . . This is how heroically our women fought side by side with their husbands and their sons."

The end of the war did not bring respite to Soviet woman.

Over 20,000,000 Soviets died during the war, most of them men. To this one should add the number of wounded and crippled—at least as many more. Over 1,000 cities and towns and 65,000 villages had been leveled to the ground, dams and canals destroyed, factories demolished, and millions of acres of once fertile land turned into desert.

All this had to be rebuilt from scratch. Vast amounts of labor had to be obtained, and there was only one source from which it could come.

The census of 1970—twenty years after the end of the war—showed that there were 130,400,000 women in the Soviet Union, and only 111,300,000 men. In 1945 this disparity was much greater; the missing men had been young, and many of those still alive were crippled and maimed, and not able to contribute their labor to the vast reconstruction job.

Foreign economic experts calculated that it would take the Soviet Union at least twenty-five years to heal its war wounds, and particularly to rebuild and retool its industries. But those experts were mistaken, just as Hitler's experts were mistaken before the war. They based their calculation on the amount of qualified male labor available—as stone masons, structural workers, welders, bricklayers, plasterers, crane operators, etc.—the professions and trades in which women do not usually work.

But in the postwar Soviet Union much of this work was done by women. There just were not enough men to do it.

And how did these women perform?

Take an extreme case: the city of Stalingrad. In 1941 it was the greatest industrial center of the Lower Volga region, and one of the largest cities in the country. It was completely destroyed—not a single building was intact, and not a single piece of machinery was usable. Rebuilding Stalingrad was more difficult than building a brand new city: clearing away the rubble required a tremendous amount of heavy labor. Some foreign industrialists even suggested leaving Stalingrad as a gigantic museum of war, and building a new city next to it.

But the Soviet government decided to rebuild the city exactly where it stood before.

How was this job done? One may dismiss this as Soviet propaganda, but only five years after the end of the war, the level of industrial production of Stalingrad was back at the 1941 level, and then it doubled during the next ten years. Today Volgograd (as it is now known) is one of the most attractive of all Soviet cities. It spreads along the Volga for over twenty miles, with magnificent embankments, streets, squares, and parks.

Women performed over 70 percent of the labor to rebuild the city. The same percentage would apply to labor throughout the country during the reconstruction years.

As the war generation of children grew up, and the women who were young during the war grew older, the disparity between the sexes in the younger age groups started to disappear. There were now enough young men to do the heavier work, and Soviet woman could assume her normal position in Soviet society.

By 1970, the demographic situation was completely normal, so we may now appraise the position of woman in Soviet life under normal conditions. The census of 1970 disclosed that for all professions and trades, women made up 50.5 percent of the entire labor force. This broke down as follows:

Field	% Women
Industry	48
Agriculture	42
Transportation	24
Communications	67
Construction work	27
Trade, food industries, distribution	75
Communal services	51
Public health services	85

Field	% Women
Education	72
Arts	42
Sciences and scientific research	47
Banking, insurance	77
Administration, all levels	60

Over half of all trade union members are women. In the United States only one-fifth are. Over 72 percent of the doctors—not including dentists—in the country are women; over 70 percent of the teachers; over 30 percent of all graduate engineers (comparable percentage in the United States is 0.5); 46 percent of judges and associate justices—and in one constituent republic, Estonia, this reaches 53 percent; 35.4 percent of the lawyers (3.5 comparable for the United States); almost 75 percent of the notaries; and 58 percent of all agricultural specialists with academic degrees are women.

There are over 1,500 women members of the Academy of Science, over 2,300 Professors and Doctors of Science, over 12,000 Readers of Science, and almost 50,000 Candidates of Science. Generally 38 percent of those with science degrees are women. Girls make up 52 percent of the student bodies in grade schools and 46 percent in colleges and universities.

There are no illiterate women fifty or younger.

To put these figures in proper perspective, remember that they are for the entire Soviet Union, including the regions where before the Revolution illiteracy among women was universal. Only in the middle 1930's were national alphabets developed for thirty of the Soviet nationalities. Among the Yakuts, for instance, before 1920 only two women were known to be literate; today the President of the Yakut Autonomous Soviet Republic is a Yakut woman—Alexandra Ovchinnikova.

Still, the country is largely governed by men. In politics,

Soviet woman has been lagging behind. There is just one woman minister in the All-Union Council of Ministers, and the ruling Supreme Soviet Presidium is still overwhelmingly male. There are only four women serving on it.

However, the general political picture is far from being completely distressing for feminists. There are twenty-seven women ministers in the councils of constituent republics; and one of them, Uzbekistan, has a woman president—Yadgar Nasreddinova. Five presidents of autonomous republics are women.

During the 1970 elections, 463 women were elected as members of the Supreme Soviet of the U.S.S.R., representing 31 percent of all members. (In the 91st Congress of the United States there were 11 women, only 2 percent of the membership).

In supreme soviets of the constituent republics there are 1,962 women delegates, representing 34 percent of all members. In the supreme soviets of the autonomous republics, women represent 35 percent of all members.

However, those Soviet parliaments are generally rubber stamp bodies convened only for a few days every year to approve decisions already taken. The real administrative work in the country is done by provincial, regional, district, city, and village soviets—the work horses of the soviet system. And here there are 923,913 women members—almost 45 percent of the total membership.

Still, taking into consideration the percentage of women in the population, women are not fully represented in politics. Discrimination?

"No," said Elena Shibarina, the secretary of the Soviet Women's Committee in Moscow when I asked her about it. "The explanation lies in the fact that all this political work is done as social *nagruzka,* additional work without pay, but requiring a good deal of a person's time. Men still have more spare time than women, with all the time women spend keeping house, taking care of children, etc. Many women nominated during elections refuse to be active candidates because of this. Only with more effective ways of relieving women of domestic work can they take a more active part in politics—in addition to their professional activities."

The builders of the Metro—the Moscow subway. (1936) The banner reads: "We shall give 185 meters of finished tunnel for May the 1st."

4.   Operation Birthrate

By the summer of 1944 the Soviet armies had advanced
to the prewar borders, and the outcome of the war was no
longer in doubt. For the first time, it was possible to appraise
the gigantic damage done by the Nazi invaders to the Soviet
Union.

Disastrous as the physical destruction was—whole areas
of a once flourishing country turned into a charred desert—
the damage in human terms was even more catastrophic. The
Nazi authorities had been carrying out a planned biological
extermination of the Slavic peoples, in accordance with the
Nazi program of creating *Lebensraum* for future German
settlers.* As just one example, fully one quarter of the population of Belorussia was destroyed. The Ukraine suffered almost as much. Though the Nazi authorities especially directed
their murderous policies against the male part of the population, millions of women were also murdered or deported as
slave labor in Germany. In addition, a large percentage of the
millions of Soviet prisoners of war were either murdered or
starved to death.

Millions of young men were dead. And how many millions of others were crippled beyond their biological service-
ability? The exact disparity between the sexes was never
officially published; but twenty-seven years after the end of the

---

* It is surprising how much Moses and Joshua influenced Nazi
philosophy. The chosen-people doctrine with genocide as the only
practical way of securing *Lebensraum* came directly from the
Bible. Joshua particularly gives a detailed blueprint for total genocide, often with sickening details.

war, there are still 19,000,000 more women than men in the
Soviet Union. The threat of a wholesale sex famine was facing
Soviet women; and the Soviet Union was face to face with a
demographic catastrophe.

This situation had started to worry Soviet demographers
long before the end of the war. Even if the existing families
were kept together after the return of their husbands from the
war, and new marriages encouraged by all available means,
the situation could be effectively remedied only if unmarried
women were induced to bring forth children.

Accordingly, on July 8, 1944, the government promulgated a special amendment to the Code of Marriage and Family, which was to remain in force, with slight modifications,
until 1970. It was a remarkable piece of legislation—and a
controversial one which became more and more controversial
as the years rolled by. It created a great deal of unhappiness;
but it served its purpose on the demographic level. Only in a
country under socialist management would it have succeeded;
and it fully demonstrates the power of socialist management.

First of all, the new emergency law made divorces extremely costly and difficult to obtain. Any couple wishing a
divorce had to go through two legal stages. Although the district court had no right to grant a divorce, it was required to
study each case and try to make the parties settle their differences and go back to bed together. If this proved to be absolutely impossible, the case would be transferred, with a good
deal of delay, to the higher regional court which could issue a
divorce ruling. Also the procedure had to be public: an an-
nouncement had to be printed in local papers indicating the
time and place of any divorce hearing. This publicity was designed to discourage couples from taking a final step which
was considered vaguely unpatriotic. It was hoped that men and
women in important social and political positions, those best
able to afford the involved expense—the cost put it out of

reach of many less affluent couples—would think twice before washing their conjugal linen in front of their fellow citizens.

The new law no longer recognized common-law marriages (as the code of 1926 did), only those which had been properly registered. Only children of registered marriages could claim support from their fathers. For legally registered children of divorced couples, there was a blanket rate of support which their fathers had to provide. It was automatic, and since the state was the only employer there was no way of avoiding these payments—they were deducted at the source. The courts had no right to modify them. Any divorced father had to pay one quarter of his income for one child, one third for two, and one half for three. If there were more than three children, divorce would not usually be granted.

The size of the divorced man's income was not taken into consideration, nor the income of his divorced wife; and the payments continued if one or both of them remarried. Thus a man earning one hundred rubles per month would have to pay his divorced wife with three children 50 percent of his salary even if his former wife earned seven hundred or more rubles per month, and was married to a man with an equally high income. And this held even if the original husband remarried and had a number of children by his new wife.

This made divorce an extremely unattractive proposition to men, and often actually prohibitive.

The results were immediate. Many couples living together in unregistered unions rushed in to legalize their marriages in order to provide their children with a proper legal status. And as the number of registered marriages rose sharply, the rate of divorces decreased dramatically. In 1940, 205,600 divorces were registered; by 1950 this figure had fallen to 67,400 cases, the lowest in Soviet history.

The situation looked good on paper, but it was criticized bitterly since many couples were forced to live together after their marriages had lost all meaning. It should be remembered that a married man as a rule could not obtain separate housing. In many instances broken unions were reestablished; but in many it led to domestic absurdities when estranged men and women had to share the same bed even when bitterly despising each other.

A heavy new tax was imposed on all male bachelors. Women could not be held responsible for being mathematically kept from marriage by the acute shortage of available men.

This took care of men and existing families. But what about the millions of young bachelor girls? Here the new law went the whole way to encourage such women to produce children, and men to cooperate with them in this endeavour.

Motherhood was declared to be a patriotic duty. Mothers of numerous children were given not only financial help, but medals and honorary titles. The honorary title Mother Heroine was given to all women who produced and raised ten or more children. Those who had nine children were given the Glory of Motherhood medal of the first order; those with eight children the same medal of the second order, and those with seven, of the third order.

Mothers of numerous children were also given small cash grants for each successive birth. These distinctions and decorations were given to mothers whether they were married or not.

It is hard to say how many women bore children because of the decorations, even though the Soviet Union is by far the most decoration-conscious country in the world. But the number of such decorated women is known. By the end of 1967, 104,000 Mother Heroine medals had been issued while 260,-000 women received Glory of Motherhood medals of the first order, 669,000 of the second order and 1,528,000 of the third order. In addition, 2,777,000 women received the Motherhood Medal of the first order, and 5,009,000 of the second order. These figures must have risen since then, but probably not dramatically so. Family planning has been becoming more prevalent in young families, and decorations have been losing their allure among better educated and sophisticated couples.

But back to the 1944 law. Its greatest beneficiaries were the unmarried mothers, and obliquely, the men who helped them to become mothers.

All single mothers enjoyed special privileges in comparison with married women. The state took upon itself, whenever necessary, the partial or even full support of their fatherless children if the mothers applied for such help. It was hoped that many of them, particularly women earning good incomes, would not do so; and in fact this was the case.

But medals alone do not produce children—somewhere along the line some masculine help is necessary, and obtaining such help was a bit of a problem in the Soviet Union during post-war years—what with the drastic shortage of men generally, and with most of them either already married or encouraged to marry by all possible pressures. This problem was solved in a truly extraordinary legal manner.

The new law, no longer recognizing unregistered marriages, also released men from moral or financial responsibility for children they might sire out of wedlock. No woman had the right to demand support from the natural fathers of her children if she was not married, nor to embarrass any man by legal paternity claims. Thus men were encouraged to enter into sex liaisons with unmarried women, even if they were themselves married, with the full knowledge that this would not entail any moral, legal, or financial inconvenience. Instead of pressing the natural fathers for support, the mothers could apply to the state for support of their children.

How many women took advantage of this unusual law to become single mothers?

An accurate figure is unavailable because many of them never applied for state help. In rural districts particularly, many girls giving birth to fatherless children still considered it a disgrace, and took care of the children on their own, rather than place their names on the rolls of single mothers to claim state aid.

But the number of women who applied for help is known. In 1945, shortly after the promulgation of the new law, 280,-000 single mothers applied for state aid. By 1950, this number increased to over 1,700,000, and by 1957 it reached a total of 3,200,000. But even this does not give an accurate number of fatherless children. Many single mothers had more than one child, and in some cases even earned motherhood medals.

In addition to everything else, all unmarried mothers were given a bonus when a child was born—100 rubles for a girl, and 150 for a boy. A seeming biological absurdity, it nonetheless appeared to work. In the postwar years more boys than girls were being born, and at one time eight percent more. Either nature stepped in to correct the man-caused damage, or some single mothers did not bother to claim their bonuses for girls.

After 1957, the number of single mothers claiming state support started to decline. Generally rising prosperity undoubtedly had something to do with this: many women were now earning incomes high enough to support fatherless children. And the sex disparity started to even up among younger generations.

In one respect the new law was quite cruel. It reestablished illegitimacy, even though this status ·was supposed to have no derogatory meaning. Nonetheless in all passports of fatherless children there was a *procherk,* a straight ink line after the word *father.* To appreciate the full inconvenience of this, one should remember that in Russian social practice (and it has been adapted by other non-Russian nationalities of the

Soviet Union) no person's name is complete without a patronymic, or the name of one's father after one's given name.
So all sons and daughters of a man called Ivan would have
either Ivanovich or Ivanovna after their given names, and only
then a family name: for instance Ivan *Ivanovich* Ivanov, or
Maria *Ivanovna* Ivanova. In social intercourse such patronymics are invariably used: a proper way of addressing any person is by his first name and patronymic, leaving out the family
name. (Lenin, for instance, was always addressed as Vladimir
Ilyich, i.e. Vladimir, son of Ilya, or even simply as Ilyich as a
particular mark of respect and affection.) As one American
visitor to the Soviet Union remarked acidly, "That's the only
way Russians can prove they aren't bastards."

So what about those men and women who had no legal
fathers?

In everyday social usage they could invent a patronymic
for themselves, and no one would question it. But the moment
they produced their passports it would become clear that they
were bastards. And passports in the Soviet Union are all-
important documents. The common saying has it that every
person is composed of three elements: body, soul, and a passport.

Before the Revolution, all illegitimate children were ar-
bitrarily presumed to be sired by some enormously virile Ivan
and were given passport patronymics of Ivanovich or Ivanovna, much to the annoyance of legitimate children with
such patronymics. But the law of 1944 had no such provision.
All children of single mothers remained legally without patronymics in their identity documents even if their natural fathers were willing to admit paternity.

It is hard to determine the reason for this practice, except
perhaps to force unregistered couples to legalize their unions
for the sake of their children. But it was manifestly unjust to
children of unmarried mothers; and there were millions of

them after the war, despite the fact that abortions were still legal and free, and contraceptives available. The biological urge of motherhood proved to be stronger than passport drawbacks, and Soviet women performed their biological duty to their country just as valiantly as they had their wartime duties.

As the years went by, there was more and more unhappiness caused by the 1944 law, and there were more and more protests against it. By the late fifties the law began to lose its demographic purpose; and jurists, demographers, and sociologists joined forces to criticize it. They were joined by hosts of divorced fathers who felt that it was terribly unjust for them to be saddled with the support of their legal children, even after divorce, while Casanovas could practice their activities with unmarried women with legal impunity. But law was law; and laws die slowly in the Soviet Union. It took twenty-six years for the wartime emergency law to be replaced by a new code.

Under rising public pressure the draconian divorce provisions were amended in 1966, making divorces easier to obtain. Now the district courts have the right to grant divorces, and publicity was no longer required for divorce cases. However, the child support provisions remained in force, and no court had the jurisdiction to amend them.

In practice, however a former wife in better financial condition was not likely to accept child support, or would return the money to her former husband. Private accommodation agreements were common, but the law was implacable; and there was nothing to force couples to go amicably about such things.

The 1944 law also confirmed the obligation of married partners to support one another should one of them become disabled during the marriage even if they divorced and later remarried. The new spouse had no legal obligation to support a previously disabled husband or wife. It also decreed that grown-up children had to support their destitute parents. All of this was designed to lighten the burden of the state, but it constrained a Soviet citizen's freedom in the area of sex and family.

The eased divorce law produced an immediate result. In 1966, 646,100 divorces were granted compared to less than 300,000 granted the previous year. Of course many were simply registrations of already existing situations.

And what about single mothers? What had induced them to produce children even when they had a perfect right to apply for legal abortions?

In 1968 Elena Korenevskaya interviewed one such mother, an architectural engineer Valentina Borovkova. Her story caused quite a stir: Borovkova not only freely admitted that she was a single mother by her own design, but even permitted her name, photograph, and a photograph of her fatherless daughter to be published—a rather unusual occurrence in a country where such publicity is usually shunned.

Borovkova, then a handsome woman of thirty-seven, shared a new two-room apartment in Moscow with her parents and a younger brother: quite a squeeze by European and American standards, but a comfortable housing arrangement in that badly overcrowded metropolis. Borovkova's father and brother shared one room, while she, her mother and her daughter Svetlana shared the other; all of them apparently considered this quite satisfactory.

"I am a single mother," Borovkova declared during the interview. "I am saying this without pride, but also without any shame or regret. Because I am a single mother by my own choice.

"Some people feel I should be sorry for myself. But why? I have my little daughter who loves me, and whom I adore. I have understanding parents not a bit ashamed because their daughter has a fatherless child. I have my friends from whom

I hide nothing. I have an interesting job in the architectural institute. In fact, I'm quite happy."

"What about Svetlana's father?" Korenevskaya asked.

"I had what is known as an affair with that man. I knew that he had been married before, and that he had left his wife. I had no illusions whatsoever. I told him about my pregnancy when I was already four months gone, and it was too late to do anything about it. No, I didn't ask his advice; I decided everything for myself. He mumbled something about this being 'so sudden,' promised to call me the next day. It was over three years ago, and I haven't heard from him. Naturally I was upset. But, to tell you frankly, now I am glad that I didn't become his wife, and he didn't become Svetlana's legal father."

"Forgive me for being personal," Korenevskaya interrupted her, "when you were having your affair, did you consider the possibility of becoming pregnant, or did this happen more or less by accident?"

"You needn't feel uneasy about asking me," Borovkova smiled. "I would have told you anyway. I never thought that it was likely that he would marry me. And I don't think I would have accepted him had he asked me. But I desperately wanted to have a child. So I thought, why not? Why not this particular man? No, it was not a cold calculation. All my emotions were dominated by my wish to have a child, my own child, born by myself. The man was no stranger to me: we had much in common, but . . . well, I don't quite know how to put it . . . I was quite attached to him, but he was not the kind of man with whom I'd have liked to spend the rest of my life.

"Please do understand me: had I been absolutely sure that sooner or later I would meet a man whom I could marry, I would have waited. But there was no such assurance at all. So I just told myself: 'Valia, you are thirty-three, you are healthy, you have a fine profession, interesting work, you are absolutely independent economically, your parents would understand, and you want a child. So why wait for a prince charming who might never come? And if he appears eventually, well, your child will have a wonderful father. And if not —you yourself can provide your child with everything he or she might need, and more."

Borovkova laughed at this point.

"Do you know why I say all this with such ease? Because I am reciting this almost by heart. I have delivered this oration so many times before: to my father and mother, to my relatives and friends."

"And how did they react?"

"Well, my parents are remarkable, wonderful people. Father had only recently retired on pension—he was a jurist, a criminal investigator. Just when he was trying to get adjusted to his new pensioner's status, I told him that I was going to have a child. He became very excited, and not unhappily so. He said, 'If you'll have a boy, you'll get a 150 ruble government grant, and if a girl—100 rubles.' Well, I earned a hundred."

"And mamma?" Borovkova continued. "Well, she shed a few tears, but then she started talking about diapers, bibs, baby things, and so on, and she has never again mentioned Svetlana's fatherless status."

"You could predict your parents' reaction," Korenevskaya said. "But what happened at work?"

"Frankly I had no idea how my colleagues would react. But one thing I knew: if I would appear with red, tear-puffed eyes and play the part of betrayed innocence, the reaction would be that of compassion and pity. 'Why, poor girl . . . What scoundrels men are'—etcetera. And I didn't want that. So I decided to go on as though nothing had happened, and then just face them with the accomplished fact . . . But they beat me to it! One day a procession approached my desk, with a man in front carrying an enormous cake. At first I could not even understand . . . It was quite a feast in my honor, and in honor of my future child . . .

"When Svetlana was born, my colleagues gave her a wonderful baby carriage . . . Men particularly touched me . . . They all were marvels of tact . . . Each wanted to protect me, to take care of me, as if I were a rare tropical plant . . . I even jokingly demanded their gratitude for giving them an opportunity to express their parental feelings without imposing any obligations in return.

"Of course, not everything was so smooth. Things were different with some of my relatives, and particularly my brother. He was insulted and angered . . . Others probably felt ashamed. Some showed this openly, while others were clumsily trying to hide their feelings. But is that surprising? There are always those who don't approve of your actions, particularly in such serious and delicate matters. One must decide for oneself, and then face the consequences."

"But don't you feel that your case is exceptional?" Korenevskaya asked. "Many single mothers don't meet with such understanding from their immediate families."

"Well, I was lucky with my parents and my colleagues. But I'm not at all sure that my case is in any way exceptional. I think that the legal and economic emancipation of women in our country has radically changed public attitudes, and this includes the attitude towards single mothers. I can say it from my own experience. Please don't conclude from my words that being a single mother is any particular bliss. Of course, it is not. I'm an optimist by nature, and I know how to control myself . . . But things might be difficult. I am very grateful to the government for handling these problems the way they are handled, and to the press for conducting such educational work in this sphere. As it is, we single mothers are certainly getting a great deal of help, both moral and financial."

"You could count on your parents' help," Korenevskaya said. "But would you have done what you did, had you been all alone?"

"Yes; but then, of course, everything would have been more difficult. I had moral and physical support from my parents since Svetlana was born. But since she was two, Svetlana has been going to a kindergarten—in our own neighborhood. I leave her there in the morning and fetch her when I come home from work. They take good care of her there and feed her three times a day. She likes it there, she adores her nurses and her little friends, so much so that I often have difficulty bringing her home: she wants to stay there. And all this is costing me 8 rubles per month—20 percent less than if I had a husband!"

"Yes, my parents have been a great help to me, but still I will be happy when I get my own one-room apartment which has been promised by the institute. Then I'll be living with Svetlana on my own, just as though I were alone. Twice now I have turned down offers of better-paid jobs because of this apartment prospect. I want to be fully and absolutely responsible for my daughter. Also, of course, one's own place is more convenient for one's personal life—and, after all, I don't exclude the possibility of getting married."

"Valentina," Korenevskaya asked. "What will you tell Svetlana about her father when she is old enough to ask?"

"That he has gone away, on business. And only because I still hope to get married—then father would come easily into her life. I am no hypocrite. I don't think that I should lead a nun's life. But now I am not alone and I must consider my daughter. I must place her interests ahead of my own. Therefore, the marriage question has a special dimension for me. Last year I had an offer of marriage, and I had been seriously considering it for a long time. But then I turned it down because of the man's attitude towards Svetlana . . . I'm seeing another man now. But I'm not in a hurry. I must not only have a good husband for myself, but a good father for my daughter."

"The last question. You have said that you were happy. Don't you feel that your child, in some measure, limits your personal life—your personal freedom?"

"No, not at all. Of course, I give her a good deal of my time and my strength. It is also true that now I'm spending my vacations with her in the country instead of going with my friends to the Black Sea, as I used to do. But my life is full. On my salary of 140 rubles a month, I can afford to dress well, go to the theater, etc. But most of all I like my home—I must be a stay-at-home type. My greatest pleasure is being with my daughter, playing with her, cooking for her. And then I like to dream about our future. I want Svetlana to be a good sportswoman (she already walks on skis even though she is only three), to play the piano, and to know at least one foreign language. We are very close, really good friends. And I only hope that this will continue."

Borovkova's interview was published in a popular Moscow magazine in July 1968, and the editors received hundreds of letters from single-mother readers, mostly admiring Borovkova's courage and candor. Few women in Russia, traditionally reserved about their personal lives, would dare to do what Borovkova did: to discuss their intimate affairs before millions of readers.

Also, I suspect, Borovkova is much more sophisticated and broad-minded than millions of other women who had children out of wedlock in the postwar Operation Birthrate. Many young women, out of sheer ignorance must have fallen victim to enterprising Don Juans who knew that they could not be held responsible for any consequences, while the girls did not know it. And if they tried to go after the man in question, they would be charged with adventurism: a flexible term applied to women who attempt to blackmail their married paramours.

Others might have been cashing in on the state's generosity and by bearing several fatherless children and claiming support for them could build a financial survival base for themselves.

Whatever it was, the law of 1944 was designed to encourage women to take up the demographic slack produced by the war. After suffering untold hardship during the four war years, the women were again called upon and they performed yet another service for their country: they repopulated it.

The war produced endless human tragedies, involving single mothers. One came to my personal attention; and because it was typical, I think it is worth telling.

I happened to be in Moscow on March 8, 1969. It was Woman's Day, one of the most popular Russian national holidays. It is celebrated along the lines of the old Orthodox carnival which took place before Lent; however the holiday now has no religious connotation. No work is done on this day except, paradoxically, by women who slave in their kitchens cooking Russian *blini* (sour pancakes) and receiving male callers who come to congratulate them. Towards the evening it is hard to find a sober man in the country, or a woman not totally exhausted by the routine.

But three chambermaids on the floor of our hotel had to stay on duty, so they organized a little celebration in their service room. They had the blini, smoked fish, mushroom and dill pickles, and, of course, vodka. They invited me to join them, the only male present, and I accepted with gratitude: such personal contacts are often more productive for a writer than prearranged interviews.

All three women were in their early fifties, and one of them called Xenia especially attracted my attention. Probably handsome once, her face was wrinkled and it bore a tragic expression—it was obvious that she had lived a hard life.

As the vodka bottle was gradually depleted, each woman in turn recited the litany of her misfortunes, as Russians are wont to do while in their cups. Their misfortunes were connected with the war—all three women lost their fathers and one five brothers as well. But Xenia's story was particularly poignant and she told it to me when the other two left the room in response to a call from the floor attendant. (These attendants are a feature of all Soviet hotels; usually mature women who act as submanagers responsible for a particular floor.)

The war found Xenia in her native town of Rezekne, in Latvia, even though her family was Russian. Her father was a mechanic and a Communist party member. Her mother was a teacher, and according to Xenia, they had a good life. Xenia was still in school, and a Komsomol leader of her class. They owned a rather large house. This was possible because Latvia had been an independent state between 1919 and 1940, and was incorporated into the Soviet Union only eleven months before the outbreak of the war, along with Estonia and Lithuania. All three republics had not been completely Sovietized; and there remained some hostile elements in all of them who welcomed the Germans when they overran these Baltic countries.

Xenia's father went into the Red Army, and was not heard of since. So speedy was the German advance, that Xenia and her mother were trapped when the Germans came in. In the wake of the troops came the Gestapo and the murderous *Einsatzgruppen,* Nazi murder squads, charged with the establishment of the new order in the occupied regions. All those suspected of Communist sympathies, and all Jews were swiftly rounded up and taken away; few of them survived.

Xenia and her mother were denounced by local collaborators, and the German police came to arrest them. According

to Xenia her mother was raped before her eyes, and she herself escaped this fate only because of the interference of a police officer who was a local *Volkdeutscher* ("blood German")
who spoke Russian and apparently had enough authority to
protect her. Eventually he came to live in their home. According to Xenia, he was a decent fellow and not at all a Fascist.
He supplied Xenia and her mother with food and, more important, protection from the Nazi police and local Latvian collaborators who were quite hostile towards all Russians. It is
only because of this protection that Xenia and her mother were
not taken to Germany as slave workers, the fate which befell
several millions of young women in the occupied territories.

And because, to use Xenia's words, "people are not made
of wood" by the time the Red Army came back in July of
1944, Xenia was pregnant. Her Volkdeutscher just disappeared
one night, and Xenia was left holding the bag.

When Soviet authority was reestablished, Xenia and her
mother were again denounced, this time as German collaborators, and arrested. Her mother was deported to Siberia and
eventually died there. For some reason Xenia escaped this
fate, and was instead sent to a kolkhoze to work. There she
gave birth to her son. For a while no one bothered her—her
status as a single mother was quite usual then. But when the
people on the collective farm learned her story, she was ostracized as a "Fritz's bitch." She was insulted at every turn, and
her son was no longer permitted to stay in the village crèche.

Eventually she had to leave; and because she had an aunt
living in Moscow, she went there, got a job, and met a man
who was kind to her and Volodya, but for some reason they
never "signed up," and eventually the man left her. By that
time her aunt died, and she inherited the room. Once again
she had a good life working and bringing up her son who had
been told that his father was dead. This was so usual that the

boy never questioned this. Eventually he finished a seven-grade school, and went to a school for automobile mechanics.

All was well until the boy met a girl, fell in love, and wanted to marry her—both were eighteen then. "I liked her," Xenia said, "and we had enough living space in our room for her—she was a student and her family was rich. Her father was a manager of a large Gastronom food store, and her mother also worked there."

But the girl's parents were not too happy about this arrangement: she was their only daughter. One day her father came to see Xenia, brought some oranges and cognac, and had a heart-to-heart session with her. "As a fool I told him the whole story," Xenia said. The man said that it was all right with him—there were many cases like that, and that this did not matter. However he told his daughter; and finally called in Volodya and told him and that he could not permit his daughter to marry a boy whose father was a Fascist.

"One day when I came home from work," Xenia said, "I found Volodya packing his suitcase. That man got him a passport and a job in Siberia, on some big *strika* (an industrial development, literally, "building"). When I spoke to him, he called me 'Fritz's bitch,' and spat on me. I ran into the street after him, but he would not stop or even turn back. He spat on his own mother, and I don't know where he is now."

At this point Xenia dissolved into tears, got up and ran out of the room. Even though I stayed in the hotel for a few more days, I never saw her again. When I asked about her, I was told that she was on a sick leave.

How many children like this had been born during the German occupation? There are no statistics, and no way of finding out, but the number must have been considerable. Vast territories were occupied by the Germans for three or more years, and there were millions of young women and girls who stayed behind when the Red Armies retreated. And people are not made of wood, as Xenia said. What has happened to these children?

Under Stalin's harsh rule, the Soviet authorities were rather merciless to all those who were suspected of collaborating with the Nazis. Those who did collaborated openly were often brought to trial and executed while the less active ones were deported to corrective labor camps in Siberia and Far North. The same fate was meted out to many Soviet prisoners of war returning home, and to those who had been deported as slave labor in Germany.

But there seemed to be a general rule to be more lenient with wartime single mothers and their children—particularly if it was proved that they were unwilling victims of the Nazi barbarity. And most of them claimed this. "I told our people that I was taken by force," Xenia told me, "but this was not true. I was young, foolish, and scared. And there were many other girls like me—very many."

Although this theme is no longer popular with Soviet writers, in the early postwar years many stories dealt with this situation. One of the most poignant was written for *Neva* by General P. Vershigora, a motion picture director in Kiev before he joined the Soviet guerrillas and rose to command the famous First Ukrainian Partisan Division which operated deep behind the German lines throughout the war. Vershigora became a best-selling Soviet writer after the war.

In his story a young Soviet officer comes home to a collective farm where he had worked before the war. He finds a girl there with whom he had been very much in love before joining the army. She had had a child by a German. The officer was broken-hearted and did not know how to react. The girl was ostracized and tormented by other farm workers, but she bore her cross with dignity. The young officer came to feel that the girl, and particularly her child, were unjustly persecuted.

No, they did not get together; no Soviet hero would marry a woman who had permitted herself to be violated by the enemy; certainly not in a novel. But the hero's attitude probably reflected the general one towards such mothers and their children in the early postwar years.

What did he do? He spoke to the kolkhoz manager, a strict dogmatic Communist, and told him that their duty, as Communists, was to see to it that all those enemy-sired children be brought up as loyal Soviet citizens. Hadn't Comrade Stalin said that the war was fought not against the Germans as Germans, but against the Fascists because they were Fascists? Hadn't he even cited an old Russian proverb in that context: "We kill wolves not because they are gray, but because they eat our lambs."?

To support his words, the hero of the story recounted a presumably true episode which occurred in liberated Kiev after the Germans were driven out of the city by the victorious Red Army.

A celebrated Soviet sniper was called upon to address a meeting of Kiev workers. He started to recite a prepared patriotic speech, but then stopped and said:

"No, Comrades, this is not what I want to tell you. . . . Back in 1918 the Germans were here in the Ukraine for the first time . . . They oppressed our people, and violated our women just as they are doing now . . . It was because of one of them that I was born . . . Well, I'm trying now to even up my accounts with them . . . I've got two hundred of them so far, but I'm not through."

There was a storm of applause.

Whether true or ficticious, this story reflected the official Soviet attitude. General Vershigora was very careful; after Stalin's death, he revised all his works weeding out any signs of a cult of personality.

Was this attitude an integral part of Operation Birthrate?

Quite possibly. In any event, the 1944 law favoring single mothers took no interest at all in the children's paternity, and insisted in shrouding it in secrecy. No single mother could legally establish paternity; and the state asked no questions. Children were one of the most important national commodities for the Soviet state during those years.

Young coal miners of the Gorlovka region of the Ukraine. (1930)

Women sorting bricks—the construction of the first great metallurgical complex at Magnitogorsk, the Urals. (May, 1931)

Ducia Vinogradova, the pioneer of the "shock Stakhanov labor productivity drive" in the textile industry. (the 1930's)

5.   Towards Woman's Liberation

There is a general impression that Soviet legislation is promulgated by the government with utter disregard to public opinion. This is not altogether correct. Before any important new law is adopted, there is often a widespread discussion of it in the Soviet press. It is also discussed at innumerable workers' meetings and during open and closed Party sessions. Recommendations advanced from these sources do not necessarily change the gist of any proposed law, but some are taken into consideration.

Before the new Code of Marriage and Family was adopted by the Supreme Soviet of the Russian Federation in 1969, and later by the additional fourteen constituent republics, it was discussed in the press for almost two years. Thousands of suggestions and recommendations were advanced, and some of them were incorporated in the final version of the code. So it does reflect the consensus of Soviet public opinion. Therefore, it is interesting to note briefly some of the recommendations offered.

Professor Mikhail Sonin wrote in *Literaturnaya Gazetta:* "I am in full agreement with the agitation to abolish the present antiquated law. It is hard to over-estimate the moral damage done by birth certificates of fatherless children having a blank line after the word *father.* The very concept of out-of-wedlock children is amoral and intolerable in our society."

Professor Sonin continued that there was an economic-demographic need for the old law, and it was undoubtedly effective for this purpose. Millions of children were born to single mothers. Then he said, "However this law had an emergency character. By 1958, many factors had already changed. During that year the number of single mothers seeking state support fell off. True, not considerably, but the trend was there. The following years showed that this trend had a permanent character. The law had served its purpose for about fifteen years, and had gradually lost its demographic purpose.

"The female surplus moved into older age groups. Women for whom the question of motherhood was very acute in 1944 were fifteen years older, and among people thirty-five and younger, the sex disparity had practically ceased to exist.

"Without any statistics, a young woman today knows that marriage is no problem for her. Besides, abortions are legal and free. Why then should she have a fatherless child? And the figures show that the overwhelming majority of children are now born in registered families. The main purpose of the law had ceased to exist.

"Why then now, when there is no necessity for this, should we allow young men to sire children, the burden for whose support falls upon their mothers and the state? (As an economist, I mention this even though the moral damage is incalculably greater.) But the budget burden is also considerable, and the bachelor tax by no means covers it. We must admit that the expectations of the legislators proved to be wrong. It was presumed that single mothers would take upon themselves the largest part of such expense. But life proved that the vast number of fatherless children were simply turned over to the state for support. This budget burden is so great that it could be justified only by the interests of the children. But the very fact of fatherlessness of such children causes a very great moral damage to them.

"Then, shall we reestablish support? Yes, there is simply no other way.

"The only objection to this is the possibility that some dishonest women might file paternity claims not against factual fathers, but against men in high income brackets. True, before the 1944 law, there were such instances. But they were very rare. Then the new law must differentiate between fleeting love affairs and common-law marriages when couples live together and maintain common households. This is a question for jurists to go into."

This article caused widespread comment. Alexander Beliavsky, a doctor of jurisprudence, expressed his legal opinion in the same newspaper: "The child-support problem touches upon the interests of very many people. Even now our courts hear almost half a million claims each year. There are many debatable aspects.

"Seemingly there should not be any difficulties. Support provisions cover only registered marriages, i.e. where there is no question of paternity. The rates are blanket and universal. Everything is seemingly correct and clear. But this clarity is often not in harmony with actual conditions produced by life."

Beliavsky illustrates this by quoting some letters received by the legislative committees which were working on the new code. Child support was the reason for many complaints.

A scientific worker from Omsk complained: "Who has calculated those crushing percentages deducted from salaries of divorced men? . . . Why do the courts have no right to judge each case on its merits, but must assess the same deductions from an invalid's pension and from an academician's salary, without considering whether a divorced mother earns 60 or 260 rubles per month?"

Others continued in the same vein.

"Alimony breeds corruption. In some cases this might be necessary, but in some it is utterly immoral. My former wife gets support from me for our fifteen-year-old son who is working. She takes money from him, from her present husband, from me, and spends it all on clothing and drink . . ."

"On my wife's insistance, I took a job in another town. She promised to join me, but instead I received a desertion complaint, and a letter from her. She has found another man, but she wants me to pay her for our children. I think that when a wife leaves of her own will, without any guilt on the husband's part, she must carry the burden of the children's support herself."

"My son's former wife turned their daughter over to her parents who fully support her. Meanwhile my son pays her 70 rubles per month which she spends entirely on herself."

"My neighbor receives twice as much support money as I earn while working . . . I see all around me that support payments are not spent as they are supposed to be. Why not set up the sum necessary for a child's comfortable support, and see to it that it is properly spent."

"I pay my former wife one quarter of my income for our child. But now in my new family I have four children, my wife cannot work, and my old father lives with us. Shouldn't each dependent be entitled to an equal share?"

Some few correspondents expressed different views. "I consider the equal division of child support unfair. When there is a man in the family he does much work about the house for which a single working woman must pay."

Beliavsky also quotes some complaints about support provisions for old parents and disabled spouses. "My father abandoned my mother and me when I was less than one year old. For twenty years we had heard nothing from him. Now he arrived in our town, and demands that I support him. Is that right?"

And another letter: "In ancient Greece a son was not required to support his father if the father did not teach him a trade. My father left us when I was still in school. My mother raised me. Now my father's second wife threw him out, and according to the law I must support him."

The support laws were different in different republics. In the cases of disabled women drawing pensions, their divorced husbands had to support them for a year in Russia, for three years in Georgia, and for life in the Ukraine.

Beliavsky comments: "There is much controversy about the rights of one of the spouses to claim support from the other. The present law recognizes this right in the case of disabled and destitute spouses; but there are different cases. Here is a letter from an officer's wife: 'For twenty-five years I have followed him from one garrison to another . . . I left school, I wanted to study, but I had no opportunity and so I have spent half of my life as a cook and house servant to my husband . . . Now I am fifty-one, and I have no profession. . . . And he told me that he doesn't want me any longer.' "

"It is difficult to say whether a spouse-support provision is equally just in cases of a wife with whom a man had lived twenty years or one year. And can we equate the rights of a wife who lost her health living with her husband for many years in the Far North, and a young girl just married who broke her leg while skiing? Family laws are incredibly complicated because there are no two similar cases. Each case provides a new problem. Does it mean that all those letters should be disregarded? Of course not. This is why each must be considered and studied carefully in various legislative committees. The law giver can't afford a mistake—even a slight error in one area may cause deep disarrangements in other spheres of life. There are hosts of unsolved problems, and millions of people are awaiting decisions of our humanitarian legal science."

All this was written more than three years ago. Did the new code solve all these problems?

No. Undoubtedly thousands of people found its provisions disappointing. All militant feminists will find it strangely conservative: it is anything but a radical piece of legislation. It reflects the historical, traditional Russian attitude towards the family as a basic unit of society, an attitude going back into the centuries when each peasant, land-bound family represented a small world of its own.

The new code attempts to give the courts and the organs of guardianship and trusteeship (formed as parts of all local soviets) the maximum leeway for dealing with each individual case on its merits. In effect, it recognizes the infinite variety of personal problems which can be sorted out only on the local level, and sets only guiding principles which the courts must follow. The main principle is the maximum protection of children's interests in all instances.

Part I, Article 1 of the code sets its basic principles and purposes as follows: "The further strengthening of the Soviet family, based on the principles of communist morality;

"Founding of all family relations on the voluntary marital union of woman and man,* on feelings of love, friendship, and respect of all members of the family free from all material considerations;

"Upbringing of children in organic harmony with social education in the spirit of devotion to the Motherland, the communistic attitude to labor and their preparation for the active participation of the creation of communist society;

"The maximum safeguarding of all the interests of mothers and children, assuring for each child a happy childhood;

"The final elimination of all harmful residues of past customs and traditions in family relations;

"The development of the feeling of responsibility towards the family."

A fine-sounding program but with quite a few semantic ambiguities. What is a communist family? What is communist morality and in which way does it differentiate from morality

---

* In Soviet legal usage this formula is used rather than man and woman.

in general? How can mutual love and respect of all members of any family be decreed by law? How does one prepare children for participation in the creation of communist society?

All this presupposes that every citizen is a dedicated communist and thoroughly understands all the principles of this doctrine. This can hardly be expected in life, and therefore much of the original premise of the code remains at best wishful idealism.

But let us examine how the new code differs from the one which had been in existence before.

Marriage:

Only marriages registered in special offices known as ZAGS (the Russian initials for the Registry of Acts of Social Status) are recognized as valid, and only such marriages automatically entail all legal rights and obligations of the partners. The so-called common-law marriages, or unregistered cohabitations, are not recognized unless they involve the interests of the children produced by such unions.

The legal requirements for marriage:

(1) Both parties must freely desire to conclude a marital union with no financial, national, religious or social considerations affecting their decision.

(2) Both parties must be of legal age, eighteen years for both woman and man. (In certain cases in the regions where this is sanctioned by local customs, this age might be lowered to sixteen, but not lower. Local Soviets have jurisdiction in this sphere.)

(3) Both parties must not be already married: all previous marriages must be legally dissolved.

No marriages are permitted between close relatives, between guardians and their wards, or when one of the parties has been legally adjudged incompetent because of mental illness, or feeble-mindedness.

There is a waiting period of one month before the final marriage certificate is issued. Local Soviets can shorten or lengthen this waiting period, but not for more than three months.

There is no charge for the solemnity of the ceremony which is offered to those who desire it.

Both partners have absolutely equal rights and responsibilities in marriage. All family questions must be solved by mutual consent, and both partners are free to select their own profession and domicile. It is unclear what happens if the parties wish to reside in different parts of the country. Apparently physical cohabitation is not an absolute requirement.

Both parties have the right to retain their original family names in marriage, or adopt the woman's or man's family name as their common legal name.

All personal property which the parties have at the time of marriage remains their individual property, as well as all gifts or inheritance which they may receive during marriage. However, all property acquired during the marriage is considered to be common property.

Both partners have equal rights and responsibilities concerning the children, their support, and education. Both have the additional responsibility of supporting one another in case one of them becomes ill or incapacitated during the marriage. As long as both are in good health and able to work, they have no such mutual obligations. But the obligation remains in force even when the marriage terminates in divorce, and the partner receiving such support from his ex-spouse remarries. His or her new spouse has no obligation to support a partner who become disabled during a previous marriage.

Children:

Article 5 of Part I of the code states: "Maternity in the Soviet Union is surrounded by popular honor and respect, and childbirth is safeguarded and encouraged by the state."

Women receive some definite benefits. All husbands are supposed to support their wives during pregnancies, if this is required by the wife's condition, and for one year after the birth of each child.

Men have no right to file divorce action while their wives are pregnant, or for one year after the birth of each child. Women, however, have the right to file divorce action at any time at their discretion.

In relation to children the Soviet legal philosophy differs considerably from that of other societies. Parents have no ownership rights—children belong to society from the moment they are born, and their parents are simply entrusted with their custody by the state as far as their support, upbringing, and education are concerned for as long as they discharge their obligations in a proper manner, and along proper ideological lines. All children are legally protected at all times from any abuse, or any harmful influence, and in these areas the state has the widest powers. At any time they can be removed from their parents' custody, be made wards of the state, or assigned to a legal guardian appointed to protect their interests.

Children have often been called a privileged class in the Soviet Union, and indeed their legal interests and rights are more fully protected than those of any other citizen. The interests of children are legally protected in all civilized societies; but the Soviet Union has brought this to the finest legal point.

Termination of marriage:

Any marriage is terminated by the death of one of the spouses; and it may also be terminated by divorce or annulment.

The divorce procedure has been greatly simplified as compared with previous laws. The courts are expected to do everything possible in order to reconcile the divorcing couple, but they have no right to force people to remain married against the wish of one of the partners as long as the interests of their children are fully protected. Incompatibility or loss of affection are sufficient grounds for divorce. But a waiting period is designed to prevent temporary quarrels or disagreements to cause the dissolution of families.

In all cases where there is mutual consent, no underage children, and the wife is not pregnant, the divorce is simply registered at the ZAGS office by mutual application of the parties, and the divorce certificate is issued three months after the original application, provided that both parties still desire to go through with the action. There is a flat charge of fifty rubles for all such divorce certificates.

In cases where there are underage children, the divorce is handled by the local court which has the right to grant it. (The two-step legal action of the previous code has been abolished, and no publicity is required.) Each case must be heard in the presence of child welfare officers who are charged with the protection of the children's interests.

If the action is uncontested, the procedure is usually simple, provided that proper provisions for the children's custody and support have been made. Here again, the divorce certificate is issued after a waiting period of three months.

Both divorced parents have equal responsibilities for the support of their children, provided that both are able-bodied. The court grants the custody of such children to one of the parents (in the vast majority of cases, to the mothers), and sets the rate of alimony payments which the other parent must pay. Payments are no longer automatically determined, but are assessed in each case by the court. The basic percent-of-income rate of support remains as a guiding principle, but this can be modified in each individual case in accordance with the parents' incomes. It can be modified again at any time after the divorce if the financial circumstances of the parents have changed.

Division of property is also determined by the court. In principle, all common property is equally divided while each divorced person retains his personal property. If this division is amicably settled by the divorcing couple such a settlement is accepted by the court.

The court also determines the visitation rights or, in rare cases, revolving custody, with parents alternately in taking care of the children. In contested cases, the children's interests are considered first. Immoral and anti-social conduct of one of the parents, failure to take care of the children, or harmful influence upon them are all valid grounds for contesting custody rights. In fact, the only reason for refusal to grant a divorce is the violation of the children's interests.

There is a charge of from 50 to 200 rubles for each divorce, assessed at the discretion of the court from one or both divorcing parties.

Annulment:

Any marriage can be annulled if one of the spouses is adjudged legally dead, absent without trace or found to be legally incompetent because of mental illness or feeblemindedness, or has been sentenced to a prison term of a period of three years or longer for a criminal offense. Such annulment is granted at the request of one of the spouses, and the other spouse has the right to contest it through his legal representative appointed by the court.

A marriage can also be annulled by the court if it is proved that one of the spouses was not of legal age at the time of the marriage, or was already married, or if the marriage was contracted as an accommodation rather than a viable marital union. The court has full powers of decision in all these matters; and if children are involved, the decision is always made with the participation of child welfare officers. An annulment does not reflect upon the legal status of the children, and does not relieve the guilty party from the obligation of supporting such children.

There is a nominal charge of 50 kopecks paid by the party seeking the annulment, and no charge when the annulment procedure is initiated by the court.

Paternity:

The present code differs greatly from the emergency law of 1944 which exempted all male parents of children born to unmarried mothers from any paternity claims.

Now the paternity of any child can either be voluntarily admitted by the father, or determined by a court at the request of the unmarried mother. All such paternity claims, however, must be supported by the proof of actual cohabitation of the parties rather than fleeting romantic involvement. When paternity is established, the father of a child of an unmarried mother is responsible for his share of the child's support as is any married father.

Established paternity does not involve the obligation of the man to marry the mother of his child or support her in any way; and secrecy is preserved, obviously in order to protect those men who might be married. For as long as a man discharges his support obligations towards children produced as a result of his unregistered involvement, his wife need not know about it. It gives an opportunity for decent men to support voluntarily their extramarital children without disrupting their present marital life. At the same time, the law protects men from any unfounded paternity claims by the provision which requires a *de facto* marriage, i.e. that the maintenance of a joint conjugal domicile be established before the unmarried woman can claim paternity for a child through the courts.

All unmarried mothers, whenever the paternity of their children cannot be determined, receive state support for their children at the same rate as provided by the previous code, and no legal stigma is attached to their status.

The children of unmarried mothers are also fully protected when paternity cannot be established. The law gives the mother the right to insert any masculine name in their child's birth certificate after the word *father,* and her own family name as the presumed name of the child's father. There is no mention of the mother's marital status, and no child need ever know that he or she is the product of an unregistered union.

Any child, upon reaching the age of eighteen, when his separate identity documents are issued, can legally change his family name.

So, the very principle of illegitimacy is abolished both in law and in fact.

Parental rights:

Either parent at any time may be adjudged unfit to act as a child's custodian, and thus lose parental rights. If one of the parents is adjudged unfit, parental rights are awarded to the other parent, even without divorce, or the child may be made a ward of the state. This action does not relieve the guilty parent from the obligation of child support. Failure to discharge parental duties, cruelty, amoral or antisocial conduct, chronic alcoholism and dope addiction, and particularly harmful influence upon the children, are all valid grounds for such action which might be initiated at either parent's request, or by the court on the recommendation of the child welfare organization.

The erring parent may be ordered to leave the conjugal domicile by the court which has no obligation to provide housing for him or her. (It is difficult to see how this works in practice since all housing allotments are handled by the state, local soviets, or trade unions. The law does not clarify this point, but I have been assured that trade unions usually take care of all such matters.)

Parental rights, once revoked, can be reestablished by

the court at the request of a disfranchised parent if the conditions which had led to the action have been corrected.

In certain cases children may be removed from their parents' custody without parental rights being revoked. This can be done on the recommendation of the child welfare offices, and is usually done on a temporary basis until a specific condition has been corrected. Inadequate housing, harmful physical surroundings, contagious sickness in the family, geographical location of the parents making proper education of the children impossible, etc., can all be the basis for such action.

Interfamily obligations:

In this area the new code may appear to be extremely conservative, but it reflects traditional family ties which have existed in the Soviet Union for centuries, and are in line with the state's attempts to strengthen the family.

The code not only establishes the parents' responsibility to support their children, but grown-up children's responsibility to support their disabled or destitute parents. It further establishes the obligation of grandchildren, and vice versa, as well as the responsibility of any person to support his or her disabled brothers and sisters, and also the mutual obligation of guardian and ward to support each other.

The legal provisions, I have been told, are applicable only in rare and extreme cases. The courts have complete jurisdiction in all such matters to protect all persons from unjustified claims, but the presence of the provisions in the present code will undoubtedly provoke many complaints.

It is difficult to see what the Soviet legislators had in mind in this area. Surely no family can be held together in the absence of mutual affection between their members, and even if the obligation of children to support their disabled and destitute parents may be justified by the fact that the parents contributed to their support and education, it seems to be groundless in the case of grandparents or sister and brothers.

When I discussed this with some members of the Committee of Soviet Women, I was told that these provisions were temporary and will be abolished as soon as the present pension scheme spreads to older age groups, those who might not now be covered by pension protection. At present they were necessary to relieve the state of the expense of supporting disabled people who might not have contributed anything to the general public welfare.

These explanations are not fully satisfactory, and I felt that this part of the code was a contradiction of the basic socialist principle that the state was responsible for the welfare of all its citizens regardless of their status.

Adoption:

Children may be adopted either with the permission of their parents or by the decision of the child welfare organization which functions in conjunction with the local soviet. Anyone may apply as adoptive parents except those who have been declared unsuitable parents. When the children are over ten years of age, their own agreement is required. If the adopter is married, the agreement of his or her spouse is required as well.

All adoption procedures are secret. Any public revelation is a criminal offense. When a child is adopted he or she may be given a new name and patronymic, as well as the family name of the adoptive parents.

Any adoption may be cancelled by the court should the adoptive parents prove to be unable to raise the child properly, in which case the child is returned to the child welfare organization.

No adoption can be cancelled once the child reaches eighteen—unless at his own request. A cancellation after this age does not release him from the obligations towards his adoptive parents which are the same as any child's obligations towards their real parents.

Guardianship and trusteeship:
There are many articles covering these subjects, but they do not materially differ from such laws in all Western societies. The local soviets have complete jurisdiction in such matters: they appoint guardians for children under the age of ten, and trustees for older children. Such appointments are always made in the interests of the children, and the child welfare offices supervise all children until they reach the age of eighteen. Guardians and trustees defend all legal rights of their wards, and the law does not permit any financial agreements to be made between them; and no marriages can be contracted between guardians and their wards.

All guardians and trustees may be replaced by the decision of child welfare organization, should they prove to be unfit to act in their capacities. The natural parents of any child have the responsibility of supporting him, even in those cases where their parental rights have been revoked.

Marriages with foreigners and marriages contracted abroad
At one time such marriages were virtually impossible, but the new code recognizes them as valid. Marriage does not reflect upon the citizenship of either spouse. And if either of the prospective spouses resides in the U.S.S.R. at the time of marriage, all children of the marriage are considered to be Soviet citizens. But when the children are born abroad, their citizenship is determined by mutual consent of the parents, and in conformity with the laws of the country where they were born.

All foreigners marrying in the U.S.S.R. come under the jurisdiction of Soviet courts, and have the same rights and responsibilities as Soviet citizens. All marriages between Soviet citizens and foreigners contracted abroad are recognized as valid, and while such foreigners reside in the U.S.S.R. they come under Soviet laws regarding family and divorce rights. All divorces obtained abroad by Soviet citizens or foreigners are recognized as valid by the Soviet law.

All Soviet laws about marriage and family apply to people without citizenship legally residing in the U.S.S.R.

The liberalization of the laws concerning marriages between Soviet citizens and foreigners does not make such marriages simple in practice. Since marriage does not change the citizenship status of either partner, the foreign wife of a Soviet citizen may not be permitted to come and reside with him in the Soviet Union, and a Soviet citizen marrying a foreigner will not be permitted to leave the country without special dispensation from the proper authorities. Such permission is almost impossible to obtain for a man; but some Russian girls have been permitted to leave the country with their foreign husbands. However there is no assurance that permission would be forthcoming in any individual case.

Family planning:

The code does not mention this subject at all. It is considered to be an absolutely private matter for each married or unmarried woman. The existing Soviet laws are most liberal in this sphere.

The right of woman to prevent or terminate any unwanted pregnancy was an integral part of the Soviet legislation promulgated immediately after the revolution, and it has never been curtailed since, not even during the most acute periods of demographic difficulties.

This attitude was based on Lenin's beliefs. Although he was bitterly opposed to the Malthusian doctrine of reduced birthrate as a socio-economic measure, he held that woman's right of birth control was an integral part of her liberation from all other archaic traditions.

Attacking the birth control symposium held in St. Peters-

burg in 1913 for treating the problem as a protective measure
of the rich against the proliferation of the poor, he said: "Of
course this does not prevent us from demanding the complete abolition of all the laws condemning abortions or dissemination of medical birth-control information. All such
laws are nothing but hypocrisy of the ruling classes. They do
not cure the ulcers of capitalism, but make them all the more
malignant, particularly in relation to the working classes. But
it is one thing to demand the freedom of medical information,
safeguarding the most basic democratic rights of all citizens,
and another to apply neo-Malthusianism as a social measure.
All conscientious workers will wage a merciless fight against
all attempts to impose upon them this cowardly and reactionary teaching." *

At present all the rules governing abortions are based
solely on medical grounds. There is no question of preventing
any woman from having one on any other ground. This is her
right; the decision is solely hers.

Because the question of birth control figures prominently
on many levels of today's world, it is interesting to examine
how it is handled in the Soviet Union. One should remember
that the spectre of a population explosion does not threaten
the country locally; on the contrary, there is interest on the
part of the government to increase the birthrate. Therefore it
is especially remarkable that woman's right to bear or not to
bear children has not been violated or restricted during the
entire history of the Soviet Union.

How does Soviet woman handle the situation?

Admittedly the question of sex education has been
neglected in the country due to traditional reticence about
discussing the subject. For centuries sex has been an unmen-
tionable subject; and even now there is little written about it
outside of medical journals.

---

* V. Lenin. *The Working Class and Neo-Malthusianism.*

Soviet woman can get advice and guidance from a network of special women's clinics throughout the country. There were 19,300 of them in 1965, and the number has increased since then. Like all medical services, this service is free; and unlike other services, it is restricted to women. Any Soviet girl or woman who finds herself in trouble can come here for help and advice. Her marital status or age need not deter her: no embarrassing questions are asked, and no pressure of any kind is applied. The decision rests with her.

In large cities there are also special clubs for young couples where young men and women can obtain all the pertinent information concerning their sex problems from specialists, and can discuss them among themselves. Young parents and newly married couples are particularly encouraged to join these clubs, but membership is open to all young people regardless of marital status.

The present law provides that any woman wishing to terminate a pregnancy must apply to her regional women's clinic whereupon she is examined by a physician, always a woman, who determines whether the abortion is medically safe. (Until 1961, the opinion of two or more physicians was necessary, but now a single physician's opinion is sufficient.)

Abortions must be performed in a clinic; never at home and never by anyone but a qualified physician. All other abortions are considered criminal and subject to severe penalties.

Each woman must remain in the clinic for observation for not less than three days after an abortion, or until she is discharged. Upon discharge she is given a medical certificate permitting her to stay off her job for a certain number of days, usually five, without losing her job or job seniority.

No permission of the father of the child is necessary, nor the permission of parents in cases of underage girls. No one is notified, and secrecy is guaranteed. Unmarried girls and women have the same rights to abortions as married women.

(It is customary among young wives to go to another town to get abortions; in that way, their husbands and co-workers need not even know about it. The administration offices where a woman is working are not permitted to disclose her secret, and her medical abortion certificate must be treated as a confidential document.)

Abortions are permitted at any time within twelve weeks from the last menstruation. In all cases where the pregnancy is of a longer duration, special permission must be secured. Since this complicates the procedure, it is under these circumstances that criminal abortionists are sometimes resorted to. But this is dangerous and a very costly procedure.

There is no limit to the number of abortions any woman can have, but a period of not less than three months must elapse between each abortion.

In all cases where the abortion is requested by the woman herself there is a flat charge of 5 rubles for the service; and the five days that she may take off after the abortion are deducted from her salary. However, if the woman's income is less than 60 rubles a month, the abortion is performed free of charge.

Since all working women are subject to compulsory periodic medical checkups, particularly during pregnancies, and all pregnant women, whether working or not, must undergo such checkups, abortion may be medically prescribed. If the pregnant woman contests this decision, she is placed in a hospital for medical observation and if it is found that childbirth might be dangerous to her health, the abortion may be performed even against her wishes.

Whenever a medically prescribed abortion is performed there is no charge, and the woman is issued a special medical certificate indicating the number of days she can stay off work. No deduction from her pay is made for these days and, of course, her job and her seniority are fully protected.

There are no statistics about the number of abortions performed in the Soviet Union each year, but abortions are considered to be the safest method of birth control. The pill is rarely prescribed since Soviet physicians consider it potentially dangerous; and the rhythm method is taught in women's clinics only when specifically requested. Contraceptive devices are rarely used, although available. However, there is one device developed which is considered to be effective and safe: a small tube inserted into the womb. This method is not new, but usually such devices are eventually rejected by the womb. The Soviet device is constructed on a reversed umbrella principle—insuring its permanent positioning; it can only be removed by a physician. It is interesting to note that the Georgian doctor who developed it credits the idea to a description of an umbrella reversed by the wind in one of Hemingway's stories. Therefore this device is unofficially called the Hemingway method.

If mandatory abortions prescribed by state doctors sound like an undue interference by the state in the private lives of women, remember that health in the Soviet Union is *not* considered a private affair but a compulsory state program to maintain the health of all citizens. All medical workers are state employees, paid by the state; and all medical services are completely free. Private practice is not permitted; and patients have no right to select their doctors. But these provisions are often violated on a purely private basis. In Soviet parlance, such violations are known as *blat,* the underground slang for any illegal pull, a term which has gained wide popularity in the country in recent years.

During the last few years, women's health has been becoming a special preoccupation in the Soviet Union, to the extent that some men criticize it as giving women undue advantages. Often cited is the average life expectancy of women which has risen from thirty to seventy-four years in the last fifty years, while that for men has only risen from thirty to sixty-six—a full eight-year disparity.

Life expectancy, however, is higher among women than men all over the world, but the disparity is rarely as wide. In the Soviet Union today 104 boys are born for every 100 girls; yet by the time the children reach the age of three, this disparity disappears. The higher mortality among young boys is not limited to the Soviet Union; and is a biological phenomenon yet unexplained by science.

In spite of these figures, the special health hazards involved in childbirth were the reason women are subject to the protective labor laws embodied in the labor code promulgated on July 15, 1970, and covering all the constituent republics.

There is nothing new in these laws: they were first drafted by Lenin in 1918 in his *Revised Party Plank* but could not be applied during the hard reconstruction and industrialization years. Lenin's program demanded the abolishment of woman's labor in all spheres where such work might be harmful, the abolishment of all night work for women, and fully paid leave for all women before and after childbirth, combined with free medical help and free medicaments.

The program further demanded the establishment in all places where women are employed of special crèches for babies and small children, and special areas where such children can be nursed by their mothers, special bonuses to be paid to nursing mothers, and their work day decreased.

These demands have been almost fully embodied in the new labor code adopted at the same time as the Marriage and Family Code.

Paragraph 68 states: "It is forbidden to employ women in any hard labor or any labor which might be hazardous to their health, including all underground work except those tasks which require no physical exertion, and are connected with medical and social services." (This excludes women from such tasks as mining, tunnel building, steel making, chemical plant work, and many other professions which, incidentally, are the highest paid. Now presumably the young and not so young women working at hard labor, who have been so noticeable to foreign travelers, will be gradually phased out of such occupations—sometime, no doubt, to their displeasure.)

Paragraph 69: "No woman should be engaged in any night work with the exception of those spheres of national economy in which this might be required as a temporary measure. No woman who is pregnant, nursing, or who has a child under the age of one year, can be employed in *any* night or overtime work, or work during legal rest days, or sent to any out-of-town work assignments . . . No woman who has children between the ages of one to eight years, can be assigned to any overtime work or sent on any out-of-town work assignments without her specific consent." (Because all overtime and holiday work is paid at a time-and-a-half rate for the first two hours and double-time thereafter, this obviously reflects on the earning capacity of women in general. The out-of-town work assignments always carry generous expense allowances, and are usually eagerly sought after by Soviet workers.)

Paragraph 70: "All pregnant women, in accordance with medical indications, should be assigned to lighter work for the duration of their pregnancies with no reduction in their pay. Nursing mothers and mothers with children below the age of one should be also assigned to lighter work without any reduction in pay, whenever this is medically indicated."

Paragraph 71: "Women are entitled to leaves of absence for 56 days before and 56 days after every childbirth with an average pay paid to them for these periods from social funds. In cases of multiple or difficult births the postnatal leave is to be extended to 70 days. All mothers can extend their absence from work after every childbirth until the child reaches the age of one, at their own expense, but without losing their employment or job seniority."

Paragraph 73: "It is specifically forbidden to refuse employment or lower the pay of any woman for the reasons connected with her pregnancy, childbirth, or child nursing. The dismissal of any pregnant or nursing woman, or any woman who has children below the age of one year, is specifically forbidden except in those cases when the enterprise is liquidated altogether, whereupon all such women must be provided with comparable substitute employment."

Of course women are subject to all other labor-law benefits in full equality with men, with equal pay for equal work, the same paid vacations, and the same pension privileges. The only difference is that women's pensionable age is five years lower than that of men—i.e. fifty-five instead of sixty.

The pension scheme in the Soviet Union deserves special mention. It is paid from so-called social funds which are contributions made by the enterprise with no deduction from the workers' pay. Another feature which sets it aside from pension schemes elsewhere is that all pensioners may continue working full time while drawing their pensions. This is logical in view of the chronic labor shortage in the country. Recently all agricultural workers have also been covered by state pensions; until then they were covered by pension schemes of each individual kolkhoz.

The maximum pension is 120 rubles per month, and it is given to men and women who work a minimum of 15 years for the same enterprise. For those who did not work this minimum time or have changed their employments frequently, the pension rate is substantially lower, with the new minimum set at 45 rubles per month.

In places with hard climatic conditions such as Siberia each work year is computed at seventeen months towards pensionable retirement age. The same applies to occupations designated as hazardous, which also pay substantially higher wages.

6. The Liberated Soviet Woman

The new Code of Marriage and Family had a mixed reception in the Soviet Union, particularly among women. It is unclear what they wanted, but many conservative provisions of the new code fell far short of their expectations. It certainly blazed no new trails toward the liberation of women; on the contrary, it seemed to sanctify woman's identification with the home and with household drudgery.

One hears many gripes from Soviet women nowadays. Woman's situation has improved vastly since the revolution, but most complain that improvement has not been fast or radical enough. True, they say, woman has complete equality under the law, and equal educational opportunities with men; but this, paradoxically, has brought into sharper focus the physiological disadvantages of women which an illiterate peasant *baba* would take for granted. There is an enormous additional burden of bearing children, caring for them, and keeping house—a burden unrewarded and, in most cases, not even appreciated. This "revolting, degrading, dehumanizing, monstrously wasteful work," to use Lenin's description, had been woman's lot in the old society. The work still exists in the life of the average Soviet woman, and it is as revolting, degrading, dehumanizing and wasteful as ever; but today's professionally educated woman refuses to take it for granted.

Average is the key word here. There are many women scientists, factory and plant managers, and kolkhoz directors; statistics prove their percentage is much higher than in most societies. But these are above average women who have achieved their position despite the age-old disadvantages which

111

their sex had imposed upon them. The vast majority of average Soviet women haven't been so lucky.

True, almost all able-bodied women work, and thus they have achieved financial independence from men. But can this basic independence be equated with economic and social equality? If one would poll Soviet women in the street the answer would be a resounding *nyet!*

Statistics bear them out. Though women comprise over half of all the labor force, men probably earn over three-quarters of the aggregate income earned by Soviet citizens. Exact figures are not available and this may be a conservative estimate.

Whose fault is it? Surely every avenue of life is open to Soviet woman. She can choose her school, her profession, and her degree of education in this profession. All education is free and state sponsored with students entitled to nominal grants while they are studying. But the statistics show a bias. While some 52 percent of all lower and normal school students are girls, the percentage falls to 44 percent at university level. And when it comes to still higher degrees, the percentage falls even further. While over 50 percent of those receiving basic technical training are women, the percentage of women engineers falls to 30 percent, a respectable percentage to be sure, but not representing the full number of young women who could have availed themselves of this opportunity. The same phenomenon occurs in all other professional fields.

What are the reasons for this inequality? The most important is the physiological function of women as mothers. The result of a research conducted by the Institute of Public Opinion, the Soviet version of the Gallup Poll, in 1970 showed that an average Soviet working woman had half as much time as a man for social activities, reading, additional education, and rest—and one hour less for sleep at night. Married women had no time at all for sports and outdoor recreation.

Here again an *average* woman has been taken, and not a mother wearing the Glory of Motherhood medal. Prolific mothers are surrounded by universal honour and respect, in accordance with the official Soviet declaration, but they simply cannot compete with men in vocational fields, despite whatever education they may have received.

An eminent Soviet scientist told me when the question of woman's equality came up: "Demographers say that to keep the country's population from decreasing, every couple must produce a minimum of two and one-third children. If one deducts the men and women who are not married, or prefer to remain childless, this average goes up to two and two-third children for every couple. But the word couple is misleading. The whole burden of the statistics falls on woman. Every time a professional woman takes off the prescribed time for childbirth, she falls behind in her skill or profession. And that is just the beginning. What if this is repeated two, three, four or more times? Again, this is not the whole story. Children get sick, get hurt, get into trouble. How can a woman surgeon perform a complicated operation while her own child is sick in another hospital? As for rest days and vacations for married women with children, those are the most trying of all! The children are home, and there are thousands of things which must be done for them, things which have been neglected during work days. I have often noticed that married girls in our institute come to work on a Monday more tired than they were on Friday night. So what happens? Comes promotion time, and they are left behind, and the men get ahead."

"Then what's the answer?" I asked.

"I don't know. The law forbids all discrimination, but that is impossible to avoid. The best qualified people must be advanced, and in the vast majority of cases those are men. Even if we cheat and let women get ahead, they are lost in their new jobs. The work suffers, and those poor women suffer as

well. Don't misunderstand me. Women are just as capable
and often more conscientious than men, but they can't cope
with their work and their family duties at the same time.
There are only twenty-four hours in every day, and with the
tremendous volume of new information, not one hour can be
wasted if one wants to keep up with one's work. Let me give
you an example. In our profession—medicine—women are in
an overwhelming majority. But first of all, this profession is
notoriously poorly paid in general; and then women fill all
the lowest paid jobs—ward attendants, nurses, midwives, general practitioners. There are precious few women in advanced
medical research, and most of them have achieved their positions by sacrificing their personal lives as wives and mothers.
This is the true story."

But many women also believe, as in our societies, that
they are victims of the traditional masculine superiority syn-
drome. "Because of their scarcity after the war, men have
been spoiled, pampered, and overvalued," a woman social
worker in Siberia told me. "They still feel that because of
their physical strength they are superior human beings. It
will take several generations to eradicate this, because many
women—believe it or not—support men in this attitude. There
must be some innate inferiority complex inherent in woman's
physiological makeup. Some time ago I watched an election
meeting in a large Omsk factory where 90 percent of the
workers were women. They were electing seven members for
the factory advisory committee. You guessed it—they elected
seven men! A few women were nominated, but they all
begged off—mostly because of the work they had to do at
home. But that was just an excuse: some were not even
married. And one simply said, 'Comrades, this is not woman's
work.' So before women achieve full equality, they must re-
educate themselves—convince themselves that they are just
as good as men."

I told her about the women's lib movement in America and Europe, and she was interested. But she thought that in the Soviet Union the problem was different. It was not getting equal rights that was important, but learning to use them. It was a purely psychological problem involving the changing of traditional attitudes. Many women were avoiding the responsibilities which Soviet laws offered them, preferring to remain in the shadow and not trying for prominent positions. "It is still the ask-my-husband attitude," she said.

This opinion was supported by an eminently successful woman engineer Vera Rybka, head of the gigantic Troitsk Thermal Electrical Complex in the Urals. In an interview with Ada Levina, she frankly admitted the drawbacks of being a woman in a high managerial position.

"You ask me whether my task is more difficult because I am a woman? Well, let's consider some facts. More than half of all people with technical education in our country are women. But do we see many women heading large projects or industrial enterprises? No, unfortunately, we do not. This means that old prejudices are still alive. They no longer stand in woman's way as they stood before, but they still act as pebbles under her feet, slowing her down. Yes, the larger the responsibility of a woman leader, the harder it is for her."

Rybka quoted another successful woman—the chief metallurgical engineer of a large enterprise: "We women in leading positions cannot make mistakes. If a man makes a mistake, so what? To err is human, only he who does nothing makes no mistakes, etcetera. But if a woman makes a slip— of course, *woman!* How could they entrust a thing like that to a *woman?* We must be much better than men, even to start being equal to them."

It is the proud boast of official Soviet propagandists that all contradictions of the capitalist societies have been eliminated in the Soviet Union. This opinion is not generally

shared by many rank-and-file Soviet citizens, and many problems which are not supposed to exist in the Soviet Union are
periodically aired in the official Soviet press. Among the topics
open for discussion is the position of women in the Soviet
world. It is freely admitted that the basic problem remains
far from being resolved, and women are spearheading the
attack. An active women's liberation movement, involving
more and more women, exists in the country.

A year ago, the Soviet digest magazine *Sputnik* opened
its pages for the discussion of the problem. Any critical writer
in the Soviet Union, must carefully watch his step, lest he
be suspected of disloyalty. Still, some illuminating attitudes
were expressed.

A well-known publicist Elena Andreyeva opened the
discussion with a short article entitled "Against Patriarchal
Views." It said in part: "In the Soviet Union men and women
are equal before the law. This is a great achievement. But
this legal equality has not as yet become actual because, in
many families, woman continues to carry the entire burden
of the housework, in addition to her professional occupation.

"The fact that the sex paradoxically called weaker has
to carry a much larger load than the so-called stronger sex
cannot but worry us. This causes far-reaching consequences:
women just cannot devote as much time as men to any creative socially-beneficial activities . . .

"Some people want to solve the problem by going back
to the patriarchal attitude holding woman best fit to bear
children and feather the family nest. They often explain this
attitude as chivalry—the desire to protect women."

There has been a great stress on chivalry in recent Soviet
official propaganda as a part of feminization of women, undoubtedly with a view to increasing the birthrate. Women
have been urged to pay attention to their appearance, and
men to be chivalrous towards them. The Soviet Union is the

only country in Europe where the old custom of kissing ladies' hands is still widely practised. So Andreyeva lets out her next blast in that direction.

"Chivalry is very often misinterpreted by us. Some think that a chivalrous man is the one who helps a woman with her overcoat. But ask such a gallant whether he helps his wife with her housework! In the majority of cases those gallant knights do nothing at home.

"Some writers propose that a married woman's working day be sufficiently shortened to provide her with time to take care of her children and her housework. But that would only emphasize woman's degrading position and would legalize this vicious situation.

"The argument that the task of bringing up children is primarily a woman's task is also unconvincing. Men can bring up children just as well. The real educational development of children depends on the home atmosphere, and a mother who is a cook and a houseworker is usually a poor educator—her degraded position creates the wrong climate for children to grow in. Not to mention the fact that such distribution of labor places women entirely under man's dependence. No, the very term 'housewife' must disappear once and for all!

"Isn't it more logical to solve the problem on the following basis: since the family is shared and the house is shared, housekeeping must be a joint task. Men can wash dishes and diapers, bathe children and dress them just as well as women, not to speak of other housework requiring muscular strength. It just must be done together.

"I want to add a few words about femininity and masculinity. Some men interpret femininity as weakness, tenderness, servility with an absolute added requirement of sexual attractiveness. But such femininity is necessary only for those men who wish to enslave woman by their presumed masculine superiority.

"The question of factual, and not merely legal, equality in the area of family responsibility affects the social role of woman in society, and her place in the family. As it stands now it is far from satisfactory.

"A relentless merciless struggle against patriarchal attitudes must be waged, no matter how difficult it may be to destroy them. This difficulty frightens many women into passivity and submission to those attitudes, even when they understand their basic viciousness, and are bitterly condemning them in their hearts."

This article evoked wide response, and Boris Riabinin, another Soviet journalist, expressed a thoroughly different opinion. "Some time ago I overheard a conversation between two women. A young mother complained to her older friend that she had to take a year off from her medical work. Her baby was often sick, it was impossible to find a nurse, and she could not leave the child at home.

"The older woman sympathized with her: 'Yes, this is morally difficult . . . Imagine, a whole year of sitting at home!'

"To give a year to one's sick baby is difficult? (And note: morally difficult!) And this was said by a mother who herself had brought up two children.

"Obviously the maternal instinct was weaker in that young doctor than her preoccupation with her career. Is that a correct attitude? Some will say, yes. Haven't we struggled to free woman from domestic slavery? Yes, but not to deprive woman of the greatest joy and the most important responsibility of bringing up young human beings. We haven't struggled to let women forget their invaluable functions as the givers of life.

"During the tender years in every child's life, the mother's love and care are priceless, and cannot be replaced by anything.

"No, we haven't struggled to destroy *woman* in woman, to abolish the precious maternal instinct, to destroy in woman that basic quality which makes her attractive, desirable, infinitely beautiful, and utterly irreplaceable. And now we are trying to violate and overpower her very nature, and replace it with something false and unnatural. This is the basis of all our disappointments in the most important sphere of all—bringing up properly new generations of our citizens.

"After all it is the home atmosphere which shapes a child's emotional makeup, just as the school develops his mind. And the mother is the foremost fountainhead of any child's emotional well-being.

"Can anyone deny that every normal woman wants to be loved, desired, that she wants to have a husband, her own family, her own home? No matter how many grandiloquent speeches we make about every road in life being open to woman, about her freedom to select any role in life which she might desire to play, all this freedom will be barren if she is forced to stop being a woman. Who can dare to deny this?

"Do we have the right to force her to do this? (And, most important, should we?) By freeing woman from all the past injustices, we are forcing her now into full participation in economic activities, at the same time expecting her to run around the shops with full shopping bags.

"I want to be understood correctly. I do not advocate a return to the past, to chain women to their kitchens, and to limit their interests by the four walls of their husbands' homes. That is an extreme. But another extreme is just as dangerous: the liberation of woman from her responsibilities of motherhood, from her role as the mistress of her home, from

her proper position in her family. A strong family means a
strong society. Without solid families we cannot raise stable
and morally dependable new generations.

"I am convinced that many admitted ills in the sphere
of education in our country are based on the fact that some
mothers begin to forget that they are mothers, start to neglect
their maternal duties, finding them bothersome. Not only that,
some regard with utter disdain those women who devote a
proper share of their time to their homes and their children.
Housewives! The word has assumed a derogatory connotation. But behind the word lies the enormous and still unap-
preciated labor of our mothers who try to discharge honestly
their duties of bringing up the new generations.

"Probably, to solve this problem, we must take some social measures to set up legal norms. I am personally convinced
that when this becomes economically possible, the state must
decree a shorter working week for women with children, without any reduction in pay. But this should place an obligation
upon them as well: to devote this time to bringing up their
children properly. Perhaps, taking the example of some countries, we should also give pay increases to fathers, thus encouraging families to have more children and giving them
an opportunity to take care of them properly, freeing their
parents from financial worries, and giving them full opportunity to devote all their attention to their children.

"Of course it is absolutely clear that woman should not
be divorced from active participation in the country's economic life. The question is: how to help her to combine her
roles of an economically and socially productive member of
the society, with her responsibilities towards her children and
her family? What must be done for that? First of all, to provide her with enough time for the discharge of all her feminine
duties, including care for her appearance. This can be achieved
by setting up nurseries, shops, and beauty salons in every fac-

tory and every office building so that women would spend as little time as possible on drudgery, and as much as possible on being women, wives, and mothers.

"The maternal feeling is, above all, the feeling of responsibility towards society, a responsibility which no one else can assume. No one.

"In this connection I admire a statement of one of my women friends: 'I need my work as an outlet into the world. But for as long as my children need me, I am above everything else their mother.'"

Those articles, expressing diametrically opposite views, brought in thousands of letters from readers—with women almost solidly supporting Andreyeva, and men often agreeing with Riabinin.

Spartak Gazarian, another Soviet journalist, found fault with both sides. "The importance of the questions raised by Andreyeva and Riabinin cannot be denied. But, alas, one cannot fully agree with either of them.

"Of course, we must lighten married woman's load. In this respect Riabinin's arguments are quite valid. But why insist on mathematically equating the amount of free time mothers have with the quality of the upbringing their children receive? . . .

"I am convinced that the quality of home education depends entirely on the personalities of the children's parents. First of all parents must educate themselves, and by so doing educate their children. A child must admire his parents, must know what they are doing, what their interests are, their activities and thoughts. This is the proper basis of a proper family.

"Some propose to liquidate all inequality between the sexes by bringing up boys and girls on exactly similar lines.

The prospect: women who are just as physically strong as men, and men who possess the same amount of nesting instinct as women. Complete equality!

"But, excuse me—what about love? True love is not based solely on mutual sexual attraction, and not even on the spiritual affinity and similarity of views and opinions. Here we deal with something else: female qualities in woman, and male qualities in man.

"Andreyeva equates femininity with weakness, limitation, subservience, toadying. Why? This is so absurd that it is ridiculous to even argue about it. There are feminine women who are strong, courageous, loyal, and intelligent. And not all limited, stupid, subservient housewives are feminine.

"It is difficult to define femininity by a set of hackneyed words—tenderness, kindness, thoughtfulness, weakness. One must find some different definitions.

"For instance, when a man returns from a long and difficult assignment, and a woman's soft hand touches his unshaven cheek . . . Or when despair creeps into a man's soul, when evil appears to be unconquerable, it is woman who rekindles his desire to fight on . . . And when the spectre of failure seems to be dogging his steps, it is woman who brings him back to hope by whispering softly into his ear, 'Don't worry, darling . . . Everything will be all right.' That is femininity, its true meaning, and its strength.

"I don't want to say that woman should not surge forward on her own, or that her role is merely that of man's adviser and helper. And I don't say that man shouldn't know how to sew on a button, wash his shirt, or cook a meal. But there are differences in the sexes' roles, rooted deeply in physiology and psychology, and no law and no decree and no new form of education can ever eradicate them.

"Now about that modish word chivalry.

"It seems to me that Andreyeva mixes chivalry with

simple good manners. To help a woman with her overcoat, or give her your place in a crowded autobus, or to bring her flowers—this is not chivalry but basic good manners. But to peel potatoes, launder diapers, and wash floors is not chivalry either.

"I think that the very meaning of the word chivalry must be placed with us on a broad social basis.

"On streets and highways one can often see all-women section gangs with shovels and pickaxes. And in restaurants, stepping noiselessly and smiling, there are men waiters. And in many stores, behind counters, one can find elegant, pleasant young boys. Why not decide once and for all who should do what work in our economic life? Why not decide whether woman's proper tool is a spade, and man's a tray and a napkin?

"This would be true chivalry.

"And then, in their own home, husband and wife should decide who peels the potatoes and who bathes the baby. Surely no law can decree who should do what here."

But Gazarian's suggestions cut little ice with the majority of the women who sided with Andreyeva and bitterly attacked Riabinin for his patriarchal views.

One Valeria Mikhailova wrote: "Riabinin tells us that working woman has no time to take care of her appearance, and therefore she must be given this time. He feels that woman must be protected, cared for, cherished and feel herself a queen.

"He criticizes a young woman doctor who is reluctant to abandon her profession. But we must not forget that he is speaking about a woman who has received professional training at the state's expense. The state plans for a certain number of specialists in various spheres and spends a great deal of

money training them. Sometimes the state gets back a housewife, with her useful diploma lying on her kitchen shelf. The
facility with which some professional young women abandon
their work leads one to the suspicion that their education was
regarded by them as something which should be done, or
worse still, as a stepping stone towards a good marriage. Is
all this so harmless? Don't we deal here with an egotistical desire of some women to feather their own nests by neglecting
their social obligations? One must think deeply about this before sending young women doctors back to their own nurseries.
The woman about whom Riabinin speaks is not only a mother
but also a physician. We all know how quickly science develops nowadays. By abandoning her profession for only one
year, she risks finding herself less proficient in her work.

"Once I also felt that shortening of women's working
day was a possible solution, but now I am beginning to doubt
it. Undoubtedly some husbands who consider housework and
child care to be exclusively woman's task would welcome
this, but it would only confirm and legalize the injustice.

"It seems to me that the most practical way to adjust the
present unsatisfactory situation is by gradually relieving working women from all unnecessary domestic drudgery by building more and more dining rooms, domestic service bureaus,
nurseries, and schools where children can remain after classes
until their mothers can call for them."

But another woman, Galina Subina, was more emphatic:
"It is stupid to even question the fact that modern intelligent
woman has not only the domesticity instinct, but also a desire
to learn more and more, and to participate more and more in
what is called the outside world. Of course, we not only give
our children our time, but we give them our lives. But we are
more capable, more intelligent, and richer spiritually than
Riabinin gives us credit for. Therefore he assigns unjust and
insulting qualities to us without fully considering the com-
plexity of the problem.

"What we are dealing with here, is the true tragedy of modern woman. Legal equality has opened wide opportunities for her but how difficult it is to step through this open door over small and large cooking pans! Consequently, she lives under a double strain: the overwhelming thirst for useful creative work, for full contact with the outside world on one hand, and cooking utensils on the other. Her soul and brain demand a book, and her daughter's torn stockings demand mending. But let us make one point absolutely clear: our modern women are not only tender wives and loving mothers but free human beings who have discovered how wonderful it is to feel themselves mistresses of their own lives!"

Hundreds of women expressed similar views: once woman has acquired the taste of independence, there is no force in the world which can drag her back into her old *hausfrau* position. A woman architect in Moscow told me: "Asking us to go back to our former position is like telling a prisoner who has served his prison term that it is best for him to return to jail where he had free lodging and food. No arguments are valid here. Historically we have served our slave-galley term—and today we hate to even think about this former so-called security!"

A Soviet publicist R. Zhukov tried to reconcile the two seemingly irreconcilable points of view: "The undeniable fact is that the two halves of the human race have never been and never will be physically equal for the simple reason that they are women and men. This natural difference leads to a normal differentiation of their functions. But this does not signify any natural weakness of the so-called weaker sex, or the natural strength of the strong one, nor the slightest greater biological value of one sex over the other.

"Male labor requires more physical and mental exertion. Can a woman perform such work? Undoubtedly. They did it when it was necessary. And yet today we have specific laws safeguarding woman's health in these areas. The law does not discriminate. It simply recognizes woman's specific physiological structure, the fact that she is or will be a mother, the human being who produces life and furnishes the first nourishment to babies.

"Is woman's function difficult? Very. Is the work now performed by women hard? Undoubtedly. But it requires a different application of her physical and psychological capabilities than man's labor. Therefore we should work not towards making such tasks interchangeable, but towards lightening the loads of both sexes.

"Now we come to the question of legal equality. Here we face a definite contradiction. Under the law, our woman has absolutely equal rights with men; but she often cannot realize this equality because of the additional preoccupation caused by her functions as a mother. The solution lies in giving to woman the maximum help in this sphere, both by social and legal measures and by involving husbands and fathers in some of this work."

This, is of course, a thoroughly safe position, but is it sufficiently constructive for the practical eradication of the sex inequalities which exist, and have existed in all societies throughout human history? I think the answer is no.

The best that can be said about Soviet woman's position is that she has made large strides towards winning social and economic equality with men, but she has not as yet won it. Independence, yes; general love and respect, yes; complete equality, no.

In line with the drive to strengthen the family, Soviet literature of recent years has been extolling the virtues of romantic love, often with seemingly bourgeois deviations. But no one who has read Karl Marx's private correspondence could say that romantic love is un-Marxist. The following was written to his wife in 1856, after they had been married for a number of years.

"My beloved! I am writing to you because I am lonely; it is so difficult to speak to you constantly in my thoughts, while you cannot hear me and cannot answer me. However poor your photograph may be, it serves me well, and I understand now why even the saddest and ugliest Madonnas could find so many people adoring them . . . But none of them has been kissed so much, and with such reverent exultation, none has been so treasured as your photograph which by no means reflects your dear, enchanting, sweet face, obviously created for kisses . . . You are always before me as though alive; I carry you in my arms, and cover you with kisses from head to toe; I kneel before you and sigh: 'I love you, Madame!' And indeed I love you more than the Venetian Moor could ever love . . . You smile, my beloved, and you want to ask me why I have gone into all these rhetorics? If I could only press your tender, your pure heart to mine, I would not have uttered a word. But unable to kiss you with my lips, I must fall on words to convey to you my love . . . No doubt, there are many women in the world, and some of them are beautiful. But where could I find another face, the smallest detail of which, the smallest wrinkle, would evoke all the strongest and most beautiful memories of my life? Even all my endless suffering I can overcome when I cover your dear face with my kisses. 'Buried in her embrace, resurrected by her kisses.' Yes, your embrace and your kisses!"

If Marx could be reduced to this maudlin state by love, what about less dedicated mortals?

Love and marriage, once rarely mentioned in heroic Soviet literature, have been more and more evident, particularly in youth-oriented writings. And even with fiction, Soviet editors are skillful in weeding out anything which might not be in tune with our epoch, i.e. the current state dicta. Typical of the new writing is a romantic story by Igor Pchelko which appeared very recently in the popular Moscow magazine *Nedelya*.

The story begins: "From the first sight he liked this girl. First of all, because she was a beauty, and he liked to look at beautiful girls even though he was weary of them. When a girl is yours, she must be all yours, and when you walk in the street with a beauty like this everyone gawks at her, as though stealing her from you, and this he didn't like. Then again, she was a mere village girl . . ."

In this one short paragraph, the hero seems to be guilty of two Marxist sins. First, masculine possessiveness, and then an unhealthy class attitude—"a mere village girl"! But times change, and what was a sin yesterday, may become today's virtue.

How effective has this propaganda advocating romanticism been? No statistics can provide an answer since "another person's soul is darkness," according to an old Russian proverb. But now and then some indications can be gleaned.

Late in 1970, *Sputnik* published a survey entitled "1000 Lieutenants"—one thousand young men who had selected military service as their career. Under Soviet conditions, soldiering is one of the most stable of professions with lifelong security, automatic advancement, and assured pensionable old age; in other words, the ideal basis for forming permanent marital ties. Also because not fewer than ninety-five percent of these young men were either in the party or the Young Communists' League, they represented the most ideologically stable segment of Soviet youth, very sensitive to the latest trends in the party line—including the recent drive to strengthen Soviet families and produce children.

The young men covered by the survey ranged from twenty-two to twenty-seven years of age; 750 of them were married, and 562 of them were already fathers. Of these young families 482 had one child; 78 had two children; 2 had three children; and 188 were still childless. (Many of these childless couples had been married for less than one year and some of

them might already be expecting additions to their families.)
Sputnik tells us that the question of marriage and family
preoccupies military youth. Whether to marry during the study
period or after graduation was discussed. The more mature
men held that the right time was after graduation, when
young men's careers are already fully assured.

The survey indicated that two-thirds of the young officers married after graduation, some immediately after receiving their commissions. One-fourth married while still in
school, and only nine percent were married before entering
military schools. Apparently the advice of mature men prevailed.

The vast majority of the young families had one child—
the general trend which has been worrying Soviet demographers. The children ranged in age from six months to four
years.

And what about the wives? In the majority of cases,
they were younger than their husbands, and many of them
were either working or studying. There were 144 teachers
among them, 114 engineers and technicians, 108 medical
workers, 48 factory and farm workers, 98 office workers, 66
worked in food distribution industries (i.e. cooks or waitresses), 69 were students, and 64 declined to answer. Only
48 classed themselves as housewives.

These figures showed that the majority of young officers'
wives have had special education and were working in their
chosen fields. The variety of their professions show that they
represent a true cross section of young Soviet women.

Sputnik then commented on some of these marital combinations, and came out with a surprising suggestion that
some of such combinations spelled future danger wherever
social positions of the spouses varied too sharply such as in a
case of a husband possessing higher education and a wife
being a factory hand. But the bleakest future was predicted

for those women who chose to be housewives and stay at home while their husbands advanced in the world. *Sputnik* warned them that they were courting marital disasters by not keeping in step with their husbands.

This is undoubtedly a very sound warning, reflecting the dilemma of Soviet woman who seems to be caught in a cruel three-way squeeze.

The state expects her to contribute to the general welfare, i.e. to work, to assert her economic independence, and to keep improving her professional qualifications and keep up with her husband. The majority of young wives do work— only about ten percent stay at home, using their full time to take care of home and children. Even this group will eventually work during some periods of their lives, if only to earn future pensions. So, as a rule, Soviet woman spends most of her time in offices, factories, or fields.

The state also expects her to produce children—as many as possible. Children mean additional work and additional worry. This additional work is unpaid for; and the additional worry, as often as not, reflects upon the woman's career.

And finally the state expects her to strengthen her family, i.e. devote part of her time to improving her home life— which again takes a good deal of physical and nervous energy. In other words, she must combine the functions of worker, mother, and housekeeper. It is obvious that she cannot avoid neglecting one of these functions, or cheat a bit on all three of them.

This situation deeply worries Soviet legislators, economists, sociologists, and demographers. Dozens of propositions have been advanced, but none seems to have satisfied Soviet women.

The proposal of shortening woman's working day was criticized because it would inevitably reflect upon her professional qualifications, and would push her back into household drudgery from which she was supposed to be freed.

Another proposal was advanced by a Soviet economist Victor Perevedentsev: to pay all mothers regular hourly wages for the time spent taking care of their children, and including this time towards their pensionable retirement. He argued that professional nurses and kindergarten attendants are paid, so why not the mothers who do more for children than professional nurses could ever do? Oddly enough, this proposition has been attacked by the Soviet mothers whom it was supposed to benefit. They felt that this would turn them into paid nannies and nurses instead of professional women. It would only further limit their outside professional activities.

So the most workable solution seems to be to increase the number of crèches, nurseries, kindergartens, and boarding schools. But how can such mass delegation of maternal duties to strangers be equated with strengthening families which presupposes close parental attention given to children?

One may well remember here a suggestion made by a Soviet humorist that the only way to relieve the women of domestic drudgery is to provide each of them with a full-time domestic servant.

Leningrad during the 900-day siege. The watch on the Neva.

Moscow, 1941. Volunteers on the way to the front.

7.   Marriage and Divorce in the U.S.S.R.

Shortly after the Revolution, in the heyday of the radical destruction of the old society, many voices were raised for the abolition of marriage as an institution. But marriage had been under attack long before. Charles Fourier, the eighteenth century French freethinker, had already attacked it as legalized double prostitution—one economic, another sexual. "Doesn't a young girl represent a piece of merchandise offered to the first substantial buyer who wants to purchase her as his exclusive property?" he asked; and came to the conclusion: "As in mathematics, two negatives can produce a positive, so in a marriage deal two forms of prostitution are represented as a virtue."

Friedrich Engels, in *The Origin of Family, Private Property, and the State,* came to the conclusion that marriage was organically connected with a sense of private property. He felt that after the destruction of capitalism, marriage would assume a completely new form. Future marriages would be based on love, and love only; and the moment love disappeared, there would not be the slightest reason for two people to continue living together. Free divorce would be an integral part of this future man-woman relationship.

The early Marxist theoreticians were bitterly attacked by traditionalists for presumably advocating the common use, or "socialization" of women. In the *Principles of Communism,* Marx and Engels attempted to clarify this.

"The 21st question: What influence would communist social order have upon the family?

"The answer: The relations between the sexes would be-

133

come their private affair, concerning only them: an affair in which society would have no need to meddle. This will become possible because the abolition of private property and the upbringing of children by the state eliminate the two basic foundations of marriage: dependence of wives upon husbands, and children upon parents. This is the answer to the wailing of the moralizing bourgeois critics condemning us for advocating the common use of women. Such common use of women is an integral part of bourgeois society; and it exists in full measure in the form of prostitution. But prostitution is fully based on private property and will disappear along with it. Therefore, the communist society instead of establishing the common use of women, will abolish it."

In the *Manifesto of the Communist Party,* Marx and Engels attempted to explain their position further.

"The destruction of the family! Even the most extreme radicals are outraged by this vile intention of the Communists.

"What is the basis of the present bourgeois family? Capital, and private profit. In the clearest form it is found among the bourgeoisie; but it finds its additional forms in the enforced celibacy of proletarians, and in public prostitution. The bourgeois family will disappear along with private property, and both will disappear with the disappearance of capitalism.

"We are also criticized for wishing to eliminate the exploitation of children by their parents. We confess to this crime.

"But, they say, by so doing, you will replace the home with public upbringing, and thus destroy the most treasured human relationships.

"But isn't it a fact that your upbringing is merely based on your society's interests? . . . The Communists did not invent the influence of society upon children; they only want to change its forms, removing it from the influence of the ruling classes.

"But you want to place women in common use!—the bourgeois chorus accuses us.

"A bourgeois looks upon his wife as a simple means of production. He has heard that we want to abolish the ownership of all means of production, and therefore he cannot separate the idea of the common ownership of the means of production from the common ownership of wives. He does not even suspect that our aim is to eliminate the situation which makes woman a mere tool of production.

"The bourgeois marriage represents indeed the common use of woman. The Communists might perhaps be accused of wishing to replace the hypocritical and hidden common ownership of women with an open ownership. But it is obvious that with the destruction of present economic relations, the source of the present common use of women will disappear— i.e. official and unofficial prostitution."

It must be admitted that early Marxist theoreticians were quite vague about sex matters. They lived in the period of the industrial revolution in England which was marked, among other things, by a general abuse of women, who for the first time in history were involved in industrial production. It was quite common among factory owners and managers to recruit private harems from young factory workers. Many brothels were operated in the guise of millinery shops where young girl workers were forced to entertain male clients at night.

Lenin, too, was appalled by this same practice in Russia. In *Capitalism and Female Labor* he wrote that from the factory workers, "the capitalist prefers to recruit domestic help who because of the monstrously low pay are forced to earn a supplementary income for themselves and their families. From these women, capitalists of all countries—like slave owners of the past and serf owners of the Middle Ages—are recruiting any number of concubines at most reasonable costs. And no moral indignation (hypocritical in 99 cases out of 100) can change anything in this trade in woman's flesh: for as long as

there exist hired slaves, there will exist prostitution. All oppressed and exploited classes in history have been forced (as
part of their exploitation) to give to their oppressors first their
underpaid labor, and then their women, as concubines for
their masters."

However, Lenin was also disturbed by the idea of free
love, advocated by many early women revolutionaries. He,
for instance, disagreed with Inessa Armand, one of his closest
collaborators, when she inserted a mention of free love as one
of the requisites for the liberation of women in a brochure.
Lenin advised her to strike it out altogether.

In his letter to her he wrote: "You say that even a fleeting passion and liaison is more poetic and pure than the loveless kisses of common vulgar spouses. And this you want to
put into your brochure. Very well.

"But is this a logical juxtaposition? Kisses without love
are *dirty*. I agree. So what shall they be replaced with? It
seems, kisses *with love*? And you offer as a substitute a fleeting (why fleeting?) passion (why not love?). So it logically
appears that kisses without love (fleeting) are placed by you
against the loveless kisses of married people . . . Strange.
For a popular brochure wouldn't it be clearer to set the middle-
class intelligentsia-peasant, trite and dirty, religious marriage
without love against a civil proletarian marriage with love?
(With the addition, if you absolutely insist, that even a fleeting
liaison can be clean as well as dirty.) And you take as a comparison not class types but a private case, which of course can
occur in life. But do we discuss individual cases? If one
wants to take the individual case of loveless kisses in marriage and pure kisses in a fleeting love affair, then it is best
to develop such a theme in a novel. But in a brochure?"

In all his writings Lenin supported the thesis of love-
marriage being an ideal form of human sex relations, as opposed to the loveless convenience marriage based on material

considerations. But nowhere has he attacked the institution of marriage as such. He supported a monogamous approach to the problem—a union of two free individuals based on mutual attraction and on nothing else. But he also held that the right to divorce was an absolute requisite for the liberation of women from their inhuman condition in present society.

In his article "About the Caricature of Marxism and about The Imperialistic Economic Theory" he wrote: "One cannot be a democrat or socialist without demanding an immediate and complete freedom of divorce, because the absence of such freedom is superoppression of the already oppressed sex—women, even though it is easy to see that the confirmation of any woman's right to leave her husband is not an *invitation* for all wives to leave their husbands!"

According to Lenin, a complete right of divorce did not mean the abolition of sexual responsibilities, the vaunted free love, which was very much in vogue after the revolution. In his interview with K. Zetkin in 1918, Lenin expressed his bewilderment at the popularity in Soviet Russia of the glass-of-water theory: the fulfilment of one's sex appetites in a communist society will be as easy as drinking a glass of water.

"Our young people became wild, absolutely wild, about that theory. It has become an evil factor in the lives of many of our boys and girls . . . I consider this famous glass-of-water theory both anti-Marxist and antisocial . . . Communism must bring with itself not asceticism, but optimism and well-being, based also on the fullness of sex life. However, in my opinion, the overemphasis on sex which we are witnessing all around us, does not bring optimism and well-being, but on the contrary, diminishes it . . . And during the Revolution this is bad, very bad. . . . Excesses of sexual life are bourgeois: they are signs of decomposition . . . The future of our youth deeply worries me . . ."

Lenin had ample reasons for his worry. Unlike Marx

and Engels, he dealt not with theories but with a realistic situation—the violent disintegration of the old patriarchal society in a largely illiterate and backward country. The redesigning of human relationships was not either simple nor easy.

"This is a slow and often very painful process," he admitted in the same interview. "Of course the filth of the bourgeois marriage with its difficult termination, with its freedom for husbands and slavery for wives, the vile hypocrisy of sex morality fill all decent people with a feeling of repugnance . . . People rise against this horror and perversity . . . But the thirst for diversity in sexual matters may easily assume uncontrollable forms . . ."

Then how did Lenin visualize the cure of the then existing orgy of sexual permissiveness which he felt was particularly harmful to the youth movement? He felt it could be altered only by a quick mass involvement of women in the construction of the new society. "We can be justly proud of the fact that the flower of women revolutionaries is in our party. But this does not as yet resolve the problem. We must involve millions of working women in cities and villages in our struggle, and especially in the task of the communist reconstruction of marriage. Without women there could be no true mass movement."

And later: "But why everywhere, even in Soviet Russia, are there fewer women in the party than men? Why is the number of professional women political organizers so small? . . . We can't exercise our power without millions of women, we can't carry out communist construction without them.

". . . Our demands have nothing in common with reformist trickery in bourgeois societies . . . They spring organically from the bitter poverty and shameful abuses when weak woman is disfranchised . . . We are conscious of her needs, we know her oppression, we know the privileged position of men, and we hate it—yes, *hate*,—and want to eliminate everything which crushes and tortures working women, wives of workers, peasants and little people, and in many instances even women of privileged classes."

But, he admitted, the problem was far from being resolved, in Soviet Russia or even within his own party: "Unfortunately, we can say about some of our comrades: scratch a Communist, and you will find a Philistine. And we must scratch them in their weakest spot: their attitude towards women. The need for this lies in the fact that so many men calmly watch women wearing themselves out performing stupid little tasks, wearisome and time and strength-consuming; so-called domestic work which constricts their horizons, dulls their minds, weakens their hearts, destroys their will-power. I don't speak of bourgeois households where they load all this work on a hired help. No, I am speaking about the great majority of women, including the wives of workers, even when these wives earn their own living . . . We must exterminate the old slave-owner psychology in men down to its deepest roots, both in the party and in the masses . . ."

It is necessary to quote Lenin extensively, because without understanding Lenin's own ideological position it is impossible to appraise properly many facets of Soviet life today. Lenin was not merely the founder of the Soviet state, but its creator. Not a single piece of early Soviet legislation could be passed without his agreement, and many early decrees were personally written by him. Though many of the early premises on which the Soviet state was founded have been modified, few have been violated outright.

There are no statistics about the number of marriages and divorces during the first years following the Revolution. Most of the church records had been destroyed, and people often didn't bother to formalize their relations: couples got together and then split. One of the most heartbreaking features of the then existing chaotic conditions was the appearance of hordes of *bezprizorniki* (abandoned children). Gangs of these urchins roamed the cities and towns, begging, stealing, sleeping in gutters and cellars, and often engaging in organized crime. The young Soviet state had no ways of coping with this problem. There were few children's shelters, and even when the militia rounded up the children, they usually escaped and rejoined their former gangs. Some of them were led by experienced criminals, Soviet-style Fagins; when captured, these adult criminals were often lynched on the spot by the infuriated populace.

The Code of Marriage and Family of 1918, probably composed personally by Lenin, set some lawful norms; but it also allowed freedoms for which the country was not ready. The freedom of marriage choice and divorce were particularly often abused. Since any marriage could be instantly dissolved, by the unilateral wish of either party, many experienced Lotharios victimized women by registering with them one day, and divorcing them the next, and the poor girls need not even be told that they were divorcees.

Admittedly such extreme cases were rare, but the new freedoms were widely misinterpreted as the abolishment of all responsibilities arising from marriage.

Stalin, who followed Lenin at the helm of the Soviet state, has been often accused of betraying Lenin's ideals. Without justifying any of Stalin's villainous and tyrannical methods, it is only fair to remember that he faced the overwhelming practical problem of rebuilding the country, a problem which Lenin often discarded for the sake of ideals. Strict order had to be brought into the chaos—and one sphere that needed immediate attention was that of human relations.

In 1926 a new Code of Marriage and Family was decreed. Its main purpose was to tighten responsibilities in marriage. Free-love unions were equated with registered marriages; and men were no longer permitted to practise love like a sport—leaving all the consequences to the women. Divorces were made difficult and costly.

The immediate result was a mass registration of previously unregistered liaisons, usually on the women's insistence, and gradually some rather strict order was brought into a chaotic situation.

In 1970 a Soviet economist, V. Perevedentsev, included a tabulation of divorce statistics for the last thirty years in an article which appeared in *Literaturnaya Gazetta*. The figures are interesting although they show only the number of divorces registered at registry offices, and not those granted by courts. Quite often divorced people registered their new status only if they wanted to remarry. Also no *de facto* marriages which might have been terminated would show up.

1940 —	205,600	divorces
1950 —	67,400	"
1960 —	270,200	"
1965 —	360,400	"
1966 —	646,100	"
1967 —	646,300	"

The 1950 figure reflects the postwar years when divorces were particularly hard to obtain, and the sharp increase in 1966 was caused by simplified divorce procedures put into effect that year.

The fact remains that despite the propaganda drive to strengthen the family, Soviet families continue to fall apart at an accelerated rate. While in 1950 there were only three registered divorces for each hundred marriages, this rose to ten per hundred in 1960, and thirty per hundred in 1966–67. This erosion of the stability of the Soviet family has been continuing. It is now estimated that every third Soviet marriage is destined to end in divorce. (This doesn't take unregistered unions into consideration, but Soviet statisticians believe the same percentage applies to those.)

The instability of Soviet families varies greatly from place to place. First place for the number of registered divorces is held by Latvia—42 for each 10,000 of the population. Second place is shared by Russia and Esthonia with 32, and then comes the Ukraine with 30. Georgia and Armenia are at the bottom of this list with only 10 divorces for each 10,000 of the population, and the Central Asian republics have only 11.

Young couples are particularly likely to end their marriages in divorce—fully 25 percent of all divorces involved people of thirty or younger, and 60 percent of them were married less than 5 years, and 21 percent less than one.

The higher the level of industrial development of any region, the higher is its divorce rate. And the larger the city or town, the more likely marriages contracted there are to end in divorce, with those contracted in villages and small towns being the least susceptible to splits. The number of divorces for the entire union is 27 for each 10,000 of the population. But in cities and large towns this figure rises to 42, and in cities of over 500,000 population to 49. Very large industrial centers are particularly hard hit: in Moscow this figure is 60; in Leningrad, 59; and in Odessa, Volgograd, and Riga, 63. In the larger cities there is a preponderance of permanent city dwellers among the young people, while in the smaller Soviet towns many of the young people have recently moved there from rural districts.

Perevedentsev cited six basic reasons for Soviet families falling apart at an accelerated rate.

1. The mass involvement of women in the national economy. The economic independence of women has caused a weakening of family ties.
2. In the most active age groups the demographic disparity

caused by the war has balanced out. In 1969, the number of men and women forty-two years of age or younger was equal. Now a young woman seeking a divorce is less afraid that she won't be able to remarry.

3. The large three-generation families of former times are disappearing. The old people had acted as a stabilizing influence; they were peacemakers and keepers of patriarchal traditions.

4. The birthrate has decreased drastically. Children tend to cement families and today's young couples are not in a hurry to start a family. Many break up before the arrival of the first child. Large families have become rare.

5. The intelligentsia and qualified workers have greatly increased in numbers. In these groups the question of psychological and intellectual disharmony between the spouses is more important.

6. Society has become incomparably more tolerant towards divorces and premarital and extramarital sex activities.

The provisions of the new Code of 1970 seem to encourage young married people to postpone having children since the divorce of childless couples is a simple matter of registration—without a court hearing. Many young couples now wait for a year or two to make sure of their feelings.

I asked a member of the Soviet Women's Committee in Moscow about the seeming contradiction of encouraging motherhood on one hand, and encouraging its postponement on the other. She explained that while the state wanted more children to be born, it should not be at the expense of happiness. Some young couples wait before having their first child, but that will tend to make more stable families. The children will be born to parents who feel sure that their marriage will last. It is better to correct a marital mistake before children complicate the issue. Woman's new freedom comes above everything else; and this is one facet of it.

This seemed logical, but then why marry at all? There is

nothing to prevent a couple from having an unregistered liaison to test their feelings with no fear of consequences.

Still over two million marriages are registered in the Soviet Union every year. This is about 87 marriages for every 10,000 of marriageable population—exactly the same figure as in the United States. Comparable figures for other countries are 71 for France, 76 for England, 88 for East Germany, 97 for West Germany, and 98 for Japan.

So apparently there is more to marriage than a mere sex liaison. Even in the most sex-permissive societies, this permissiveness does not seem to affect the marriage rate significantly.

Within the Soviet Union, marriage figures vary greatly from place to place. The greatest number are registered in newly-developed parts of Siberia, with far Kamchatka leading all other regions with 130 marriages yearly in 10,000. The explanation is simple: thousands of young people move there annually. The new city of Bratsk, near the gigantic hydroelectric development in Eastern Siberia, leads the Soviet Union in both marriages and births.

The Soviet sociologist Professor Anatoly Kharchev conducted a poll of eight hundred couples who were receiving their marriage certificates at the Leningrad Wedding Palace. The couples represented a cross-section of the population of a large industrial and cultural center, with students and qualified workers predominating.

The question posed was: "What in your opinion is the requisite for a happy and stable marriage?"

Not unexpectedly, 76.2 percent chose love or love combined with similarity of interests and tastes, mutual trust, and sincerity; 13.2 percent indicated equality and mutual respect; 4 percent love and good housing conditions; 1.6 percent love and good economic conditions; 0.6 percent having children; and 0.2 percent a realistic outlook on life. The remaining 4.2

percent declined to answer. But, as Kharchev points out, even if these don't know's consider material factors as the main requisite, the total number of such materialists would represent only 10 percent.

Almost all those polled indicated that economic conditions were important to some degree, but were not the predominating factor. Basic economic security is taken for granted by young Soviet people, and there are very few people who could be classed as good matrimonial catches in the economic sense.

Another common denominator was that the age difference between bridegroom and bride was slight—not over three years; and in many cases, there was no difference at all.

This has been the general trend in the Soviet Union since the Revolution. Before the Revolution, traditionally men married women who were at least ten years younger, particularly in villages. But already in 1920 the number of men who were seven years older than their wives fell to 23.5 percent in cities and 56.5 percent in villages. By 1940 this disparity had shrunk to 16.5 percent and 23 percent respectively. Today in 66 percent of all cases in cities and villages this age difference is less than three years.

The main factor is the increased age of brides. In large cities more girls are studying in universities, colleges, and other schools of higher learning, and prefer to marry after receiving their professional diplomas and securing their first jobs. For instance in Kiev only 5.5 percent of the brides were twenty or younger, while in some provincial towns in Siberia, 16 percent were.

Today 21 percent of all brides in large cities and 16.5 percent in rural regions are thirty-three or older, while in old Russia unmarried women of thirty were considered hopeless old maids, with practically no chance to marry.

Even in the Central Asian republics and the Caucasus,

where child brides were once common, and where girls of sixteen are permitted to marry today, the percentage of young
brides has been shrinking. In Uzbekistan, for instance, 35
percent of the brides were eighteen or younger in 1937. The
percentage had shrunk to 12.8 by 1957; and the present percentage is estimated at 5 to 8, and is expected to continue to
diminish.

Before the Revolution an overwhelming number of married couples came from the same town or village, but the
mobility of the population in postwar years and mass urbanization have changed this situation. Now the majority of
those prospective spouses come from different localities.

How do Soviet young people meet one another?

The same Leningrad poll gave the following results: 27.2
percent of the couples met in recreational centers frequented
by young people; 21 percent at work; 17.5 percent in schools;
9 percent had known each other since childhood; 5.7 percent
during parties at home; 5.2 percent through common friends;
and 5 percent while on vacations.

The number of binational * marriages has also been
growing. In tsarist Russia marriages between Christians and
non-Christians were forbidden, and the religious restrictions
in Moslem and Jewish communities were just as strict. Such
religious restrictions no longer exist, but traditional *mores* do
remain strong in some of the Soviet nations. In the thoroughly
Russian cities of Moscow and Leningrad some 17 percent of
all marriages are between people of different nationalities, in
Taskent and Samarkand this figure rises to 20 percent, and
in Baku to almost 30 percent. Statisticians conclude this affects the stability of such marriages very slightly if at all.

The ever-growing mass mobility of Soviet young people
gives them wide opportunity to be selective in his or her mari-

---

* Ed. note: Refers to various Soviet nations.

tal choice; but it also increases the number of snap decisions based on short acquaintance. The prescribed thirty-day waiting period before the issue of a marriage certificate is designed to remedy this situation.

Still 9 percent of the polled couples knew one another since childhood, 9.1 percent knew one another for from five to eight years, 14.8 percent from three to five years; 25.6 percent from two to three years, and 23 percent for over one year. Only 18.5 percent had known each other for less time. However, the percentages are for couples who received their marriage certificates and exclude those who changed their minds during the waiting period.

A rather long—two years or more—acquaintance before marriage seems to be the rule. And yet the divorce rate is very high and growing. Today one in every three Soviet marriages are likely to end in divorce, a higher rate than in any other country.

In the United States, one marriage in four ends in divorce; in Eastern Germany and Yugoslavia, one in seven to eight marriages; in France and East Germany, one in eleven marriages; and in Japan, one in thirteen marriages.

The above statistics do not reflect the number of marriages which have in *fact* fallen apart, and where estranged couples are deterred from divorce either by religious traditions (in Poland and France) or by economic considerations, as in most of the Western countries. But then, neither does the number of the registered Soviet divorces reflect the families which have fallen apart but choose to keep the legal ties.

Undoubtedly Soviet women's economic independence plays an overwhelming part in the overall divorce statistics in the Soviet Union. Their moral emancipation is another factor —the number of remarriages proves this. Many women simply exchange one marriage for another—traditionally only the man's privilege before the revolution. Now about forty-

five percent of the young divorced women remarry, even
though the overall picture of all age groups is smaller.

What are the main reasons for Soviet marriages breaking up? The answers are difficult to obtain. Few people wish
their private lives to be aired in public; and the motives cited
in divorce petitions do not always indicate the real reasons.

Still a poll conducted by *Nedelya* of 500 divorcing couples in Leningrad who indicated their willingness to discuss
their private cases may be revealing. Fifty-nine percent were
men and women of thirty years or older. Every fifth couple
had lived together for over ten years, and every fourth, between five and ten years. Only 20 percent had lived together
for less than one year.

Each person was asked to indicate three reasons which,
in his or her opinion, had led to the failure of the marriage.
The pollsters asked whether the spiritual, physiological or
economic aspect of the marriage was most to blame for the
break. The majority indicated the disappearance of spiritual
harmony between the spouses as the main factor: 66 percent
of men and 74 percent of women.

The reasons were often formulated as the absence of
common views and interests, incompatibility, absence of love,
insufficient interest of the other spouse in family, infidelity,
drunkenness, and cruelty.

When asked "What was the deciding factor when marrying your spouse?" the overwhelming number of polled couples (59.5 percent) felt spiritual considerations were most
important: love, spiritual affinity, responsibility towards a future child. Responses were almost identical with the poll conducted among marrying couples.

However, economic and housing considerations were
paramount to 7 percent, and almost 6 percent answered that
legal marriage was necessary. These responses could mean
several things. Those having an unregistered affair might ob-

tain housing preference by formalizing their relationship. In some cases unregistered love affairs might have been embarrassing for those in public view. Family pressure could also explain why the formalized marriage could become important.

Over 60 percent of the respondents felt theirs had been a true love union; and only 3.6 percent were indifferent or did not love their former spouse before the marriage. However almost 15 percent failed to answer this question.

The divorcing men had valued sociability and congeniality of their future wives more than anything else. Almost 15 percent listed those qualities; 12 percent listed, each, kindness, domesticity, sincerity and modesty. Among women, kindness, sensitivity and attentiveness led the list, each with 16 percent; then congeniality and sincerity.

Masculinity or femininity was the first choice of 8 percent of the respective groups; while intelligence was paramount for 6 percent of both the men and women. It is interesting to note that such an obvious reason as sexual attraction was not even mentioned. However this was probably taken for granted, since an overwhelming percentage of those polled admitted love as the reason for their marriage. And the word "love" is generally used as a euphemism for sex in the Soviet parlance. Sex appeal is usually translated as *oboyannye* (ability to enchant).

Asked what qualities were now missing in the former spouse, the main complaint was the lack of sensitivity and attentiveness.

The answer to "Did your spouse ever give in to you during arguments?" was the same for both men and women: always—14 percent; sometimes—almost 59 percent; and never —about 30 percent.

To "Did you consult your spouse about various domestic problems?" the answers were: always—46 percent; sometimes—over 41 percent; and never—12 percent. These last responses need no commentary. It is obvious that families where the partners could not or would not give in during arguments, or consult one another about domestic problems, were doomed to failure from the very beginning.

Every fifth person considered the continuation of married life impossible because of the chronic drunkenness of the spouse. Another common complaint was poor housing conditions. And 41 percent admitted having quarrels or disagreements with their spouse's parents.

In interesting contrast to the Marriage Palace poll, in more than half of the failed marriages the partners had known each other before their marriage for less than one year, and ten couples listed several days in answer to the question. Of the failures 33.5 percent had been married less than six months; 24.5 percent between six months and one year; 23.5 percent from one to two years; and only 18.5 percent over two years.

The poll conducted by *Nedelya* covered personal reasons for each divorce rather than legal motives which were cited in divorce petitions.

But since the law requires the divorcing parents to state a motive for wishing to terminate their marriage, the motives cited by the divorcing couples are interesting. They at least can be accurately ascertained.

Professor Kharchev studied one thousand divorce cases heard by the Leningrad courts, and tabulated the legal motives. In divorce petitions filed by women, 29.2 percent cited husbands' drunkenness; 26.6 percent, rudeness and cruelty; 15 percent, infidelity; 12.4 percent, the loss of former affection for the husbands; 9 percent, incompatibility; 3 percent, incarceration of husbands for criminal offenses; 1.4 percent, love for another man; and 1 percent, the lack of sexual gratification. Other motives (sterility of husbands, unwillingness of them to have children, excessive jealousy, illness, etc.) were reported by 2.4 percent.

For men the percentages were slightly different: 30.5 percent cited incompatibility; 24.5 percent, the loss of former affection for their wives; 15.5 percent, wives' infidelity; 12.3 percent, love for another woman; 7 percent, unfriendly attitudes of wives; 2.5 percent, quarrels with wives' mothers; 2.5 percent, wives' sterility; 2.2 percent, lack of sexual gratification; 1.7 percent, groundless and excessive jealousy; and 1.3 percent, other reasons (such as illness of wives, drunkenness, bad housing conditions, etc.).

N. Soloviev, a Soviet doctor of philosophy writing in *Literaturnaya Gazetta,* summarized these findings. "All multiple reasons which cause our families to fail can be placed into three principal categories: incompatibility, drunkenness, and a lack of serious attitudes towards marriage and family."

He felt that both incompatibility and drunkenness were very flexible definitions, but lack of a serious attitude towards marriage and family was more specific and, unfortunately, widespread. In Vilnius, for instance, every ninth couple filing a marriage petition fails to come back for their certificate. "They have changed their mind," say the registry workers.

Soloviev makes several suggestions to correct this situation.

"It would be useful to revive the old and noble tradition of an official engagement with the compulsory publication of bans; and instead of the present thirty-day waiting period to extend it to six months.

"It would be useful to establish an institution of special marriage consultants in conjunction with each marriage registration office who could instruct the prospective spouses about the various problems of their future family lives.

"It would also be useful to include in all school curricula a special course of domestic science, where girls and boys could be taught the responsibilities of marriage, intricacies of domestic economics, methods of analyzing mutual relationships in family, etc."

What Soloviev wanted to bring up without using actual words is the necessity of proper sex education on all levels starting with primary schools. This is a glaring deficiency in Soviet education. A surprising number of Soviet girls are naive in those matters; and when they get their education, it usually comes from the wrong sources. False prudery is still one of the striking facets of Soviet society, particularly at all official levels. Discussion of physiological facets of sex are almost totally limited to medical journals, and such things as sex deviation are never discussed in print anywhere. The lack of proper and frank sex education is still a very serious sociological problem in Soviet society, particularly in rural regions.

The most vicious destroyer of Soviet marriages is drunkenness. It had been a problem in Russia for centuries, but seems to be even more widespread today than before the Revolution. In this respect Lenin was certainly wrong when he prophesized to K. Zetkin that "the proletariat doesn't require intoxication to stun or stimulate it. It does not require stimulation by sex, nor by alcohol. It derives its stimulation from its class struggle, from the communist ideal."

And today a Soviet woman, well educated and economically independent from her husband, simply will not stand for a husband's drunken excesses which uneducated and dependent woman had to accept. Fully 55.8 percent of all divorce complaints of women cite their husbands' drunkenness, rudeness, and cruelty (the last two partly caused by drunkenness) as reasons for wanting to leave them. And one can hardly blame them since drunkenness among Russian men often assumes the most unpleasant and violent forms.

Housing conditions probably come next. Despite a tremendous volume of building, Soviet domestic life still does not provide sufficient privacy for people living together. As families grow, the squeeze becomes tighter since it is difficult to secure additional living space.

One man declared in 1968 during the divorce proceedings of his son: "My son married, and his wife came to live in our single room. Every time I came home, they were making love. This was very upsetting." (It must have been—particularly for young lovers!)

The disappearance of religious brakes makes Soviet families less stable than before. But then religious dogma which kept people together when all reasons of their being together disappeared are a questionable blessing. They improve divorce statistics on paper, but hardly contribute to marital happiness.

Finally, there is an infinite list of reasons why Soviet couples seek termination of their marriages; no statistics are dependable. In all probability, the reasons for Soviet families breaking up are no different from the reasons in any other society.

But children can be singled out as the thing that most keeps Soviet families together when the original electric current between man and woman becomes exhausted.

Love of children has been traditionally, and is now, extremely strong among the Russians—as well as most of the other nationalities living in the Soviet state.

A mail call at a Siberian lumber camp deep in the trackless taiga. Almost all post office workers, including mail carriers, are women. Young Russian women are surprisingly feminine, well-groomed and attractive despite heavy work which many of them are doing. These girls are the Komsomol (The Young Communists' League) members who have volunteered to work in Siberia.

This little charmer faces a charmed future. Children are the most privileged "class" in Russia, and being a girl is still another advantage. "We produce everything men produce," one woman told the author, "and in addition, we produce the most precious commodity of all—new people."

8.   To Beget or Not to Beget?

Oddly enough, I first heard the question, "To beget or not to beget?" in Moscow—and in Russian! Shakespeare is extremely popular there, and a pun works in Russian just as well, or just as badly, as in English. *"Rodit' il' neh rodit'—vot v chem vapros?"*

But pun or no, this is a question currently discussed by millions of Soviet women. The state needs children. But women need free time to rest after their working day, or time to go to the theater, cinema, sport events, or to study. And nothing throws woman's life more out of balance than children—particularly, several of them.

Soviet women have been more and more reluctant to change the fruits of advanced civilization for the glory of motherhood. The birthrate has been steadily declining in the country; and this worries Soviet demographers more than any population explosion. While the entire world seems to be terror-stricken by the world's swiftly growing population, the Soviet Union is trying to increase the productivity of its women.

There are several reasons for this.

Some are purely local. The Soviet Union is an enormous country, very thinly populated. Taking into consideration Siberia and the Far North, the population density works out at little more than one person per square kilometer. The increase of population registered in the Soviet Union during the last fifty years can largely be charged to the extended longevity of its people—the average life expectancy has risen from thirty-two years to seventy. A large segment of the popu-

155

lation is non-productive: children and young people still studying, or old people in retirement.

The Soviet Union is also extremely rich in natural resources, still largely unexplored and unexploited. There is a chronic shortage of workers of all categories; and as industry develops, this shortage becomes more and more acute. The present Five Year Plan presupposes greatly increased productivity rather than a significant increase in the number of workers. So there is no real prospect of women being released from productive work, or even of shortening their workday.

Other reasons are geopolitical and ethnic. The presence of tremendous, sparsely populated territories, rich in all natural resources, and lying directly north of China which is bursting with overpopulation, is a politically unhealthy situation. It cannot but worry the Soviet leadership.

The ethnic situation is also not properly balanced. The increase of the Russian and Slav population, traditionally the mainstay of the state, has been lagging far behind the non-Slav groups. Though every nation is presumed to be equally valuable for the Soviet state, in reality this represents a certain danger. The Slavs have traditionally been the leading ethnic force, and the most stable one. If the current trends continue they could cease to be a majority.

The recent demographic history of the Soviet Union can be summarized briefly. During the last fifty years the population of the Soviet Union increased by 45 percent. In the same period, the population of Germany increased 20 percent, France 28 percent, Great Britain 40 percent, Japan 79 percent, the United States 94 percent, India 104 percent, and Brazil 200 percent.

Some two million Russian soldiers and officers lost their lives in the First World War. But by 1917, the population of Russia (within the present borders of the Soviet Union) stood at about 163 million. The subsequent civil war, blockade, epidemics, failing crops, and famines cost the country countless other lives.

In the first half of 1941, the Soviet Union had 199 million inhabitants. But during four years of war against Hitler's Germany the Soviet people lost over 20 million lives. The birthrate went down sharply. Had it not been for the war, the population of the country would have reached 212 million by 1945; while in reality, five years after the war, in 1950, the figure stood at only 180 million. Only in 1956 was the prewar population figure reached. Ten years later it had risen to 232 million.

From 1960, the decreased numbers of births in the postwar years began to show. The children of the war years had reached maturity, and their small number affected the birthrate. The annual population increase fell from 1.7 percent in 1950–60 to 1.1 percent in 1965. The echo of the war continues to affect the demographic figure.

In 1968 the Central Statistical Office, predicted that the Soviet people would reach 280 million mark by 1980, and 350 million by the year 2000. These estimates have been considerably revised in the light of the census figures of 1969. Annual population growth is not expected to pass one percent, and it may well stay below this figure, should Soviet women limit their families to a maximum of two children, the present norm in urban centers.

With its tremendous open spaces, enormously rich natural resources, and steadily developing economy, "the Soviet Union does not as yet face the problem of limiting its population. But the situation may not remain unchanged forever." In the light of the world's demographic picture, the Soviet Union might eventually find itself in a demographic squeeze.

According to U.N. data, the tempo of world population increase during the last quarter of this century may reach the annual figure of 2.6 percent, which will mean that the world's population will be doubled in the next 27 years. The swiftest population increase during the last 10–15 years have been registered in parts of Central America and Asia, and Albania. In many countries, the annual population growth already exceeds 3 percent.

Professor Bestujev-Lada extrapolated these disturbing figures in his book, *The Contours of the Future:* "If within the next 30-odd years the population of the earth reaches 6–7 billion, this will mean that the average density of the population will reach some fifty people per square kilometer (not counting the Arctic and Antarctic regions). Man will have to say goodbye to wide open spaces, plains, and forests, and go into the way of life characteristic of the most densely populated European countries. And if the population of the world reaches 100 billion (which may happen by 2300), and if the entire surface of the earth, including even the Arctic and Antarctic regions, seas, and oceans, is counted, the mean density will reach that of present large cities."

However, some Soviet scientists deny the reality of this danger. Academician A. Strumilin, writing in *Literaturnaya Gazetta* advanced the theory that what the world faces is not overpopulation but rather the shortage of available labor for future development. He explained that the world population density of 50 people per square kilometer, predicted for the year 2,000, is even now greatly exceeded in many countries. In 1965, France had 88 people for each square kilometer; Great Britain, 222; Japan, 264; and the Netherlands and Belgium, over 300. And none of these countries would change places with African countries counting only two people for each square kilometer.

Universally, with the increase of prosperity, the birthrate decreases. In the Soviet Union it is 40 percent of that in tsarist Russia of 1913. In the last fifty years, in Italy the birthrate decreased by 37 percent; in Great Britain, by 22 percent; in the United States, by 15 percent.

Strumilin theorized, "The continued decrease of the birthrate may present the world with another problem: instead of the frightening increase of hungry mouths we may face the shortage of available labor.

"Until now the Soviet Union did not experience this problem because with the decreasing birthrate we have witnessed the even swifter increase of life expectancy. (This is a universal picture and the population increase figures depend largely on much extended longevity.) * But longevity has its limits, and we may be approaching this limit. During 1960–65, mortality in the Soviet Union had even risen slightly—from 71 for 10,000 people in 1960 to 73 in 1965. (The corresponding figures of 1958 were 75 in Japan, 89 in Finland, 95 in the United States, 112 in France and 117 in Great Britain.) But the birthrate continued to decrease. From the above we can surmise how realistic the fears are of certain authors who speak about the doubling of the world's population during the next thirty-five years!

"In his day, Malthus theorized that the population increased in geometrical proportion while the food production increases in arithmetic proportion, i.e. much slower. According to him, a universal famine was inevitable, and wars, epidemics and mass catastrophes serve as regulating factors. Malthus' law has proved to be wrong on two counts. First, due to the improvement of technology, food production has increased faster than the population growth, and secondly, because such population increase is not proceeding in any geometrical proportion.

"The real situation is as follows. Increased longevity

---

* Eds. note: largely through reduced infant mortality.

throughout the world adds to the number of the aged, who are no longer biologically productive, while the number of young people decreases. This will lead to a decrease in the number of children born for every 1000 people. This effect of structural changes is not as yet fully realized by demographers.

"Therefore, I consider the danger of over-population to be unrealistic."

Obviously Strumilin's theory has many flaws. First of all, he does not take into account the progress of automatization in all technological fields, making labor more and more productive. Neither does he consider the demographic unbalance in the world, with some regions bursting with population while others are barely populated. This creates potentially dangerous political situations. The situation is of special interest for the Soviet Union with its practically unpopulated areas (in parts of Yakutia, for instance, there is only one person for each fifty square kilometers!) and its tremendous still unexploited and even unexplored natural resources.

In the same *Literaturnaya Gazetta,* Dr. Eduard Arab-Ogly presented an opposing picture: "The so-called geometrical progression of Malthus offers no cause for pessimism. But the theoretical calculations of Academician Strumilin offer a very problematic reason for optimism.

"The swift population increase is an uncontestable fact which, in all probability, will continue for the next few decades. Each society must make a choice: does it prefer to have increased prosperity for its constant population, or maintain the present prosperity level for the ever increasing number of people. The same pudding cannot be eaten twice under two different names.

"The investment problem is particularly acute in the developing countries where one and one-half billion people refuse to accept the present level of poverty, hunger and ignorance, and where the population increases by 50 million annually. The governments of those countries are constantly trying to solve mathematical brain-twisters: to invest capital in increased agriculture to maintain the level of food production, or to develop even the most rudimentary industry to employ as many idle workers as possible, or to increase the productivity of present labor, accepting the present level of unemployment.

"Of course it is very interesting to argue how many people our earth can feed—50 or 100 billion, during the next century, taking into consideration the swift development of science and technology. As if by accepting one of the above figures, we could solve the demographic problems of this century.

"The real optimism can be based on the assurance that humanity will find a way to control all the elemental processes, including the demographic ones, and, using Engels' phraseology, will 'regulate the production of people just as it will regulate the production of all other commodities.'

"The difference between the neo-Malthusians and the Marxists lies not in the fact that the first advocated birth control, and the second flatly deny its necessity. The difference lies in the social application of such measures. The Marxists hold that birth control is not the panacea for economic and social ills. At the same time scientific population control with the stimulation of birthrate in some areas, and its logical limitation in others, may serve as a very important secondary method of speeding up social progress."

Of course, Arab-Ogly, as all Marxists, considers socialism as the only unfailing method for social progress, and birth control as only secondary. The Malthusians, however, hold that birth control can well solve many evils of the present society without resorting to drastic revolutionary social changes.

Another Soviet economist P. Podyachikh denied all effects of birth control measures advocated by modern demographers: "Birth control methods for the solution of demographic problems may, under certain conditions, play some positive part but only as a supporting measure, and only in those areas where the cultural level of the population is sufficiently high. Even Engels wrote that increased education was the only way to curb the human instinct of reproduction. Therefore, to teach birth control methods to an illiterate population is unrealistic.

"During the World Demographic Conference in Belgrade, the representative of India, M. B. Raman, pointed out that 87% of all Indian women were illiterate, and that the vast majority of those questioned expressed their opposition to birth control and even their great repugnance to the very idea. However, in those areas where the cultural level of the population increases, the population itself begins to exercise birth control measures.

"Some authors cite the example of Japan as proof that government birth control policies bring results. But in fact the situation has been created there by socio-economic progress, and first of all, by industrial growth, the growth of cultural level, and the large involvement of women in the economy. And as concerns government measures, they, according to some witnesses, were limited to supplying people with contraceptives where there appeared a public demand for them.

Economist Podyachikh then cited the position of the Soviet Union in regard to population problems in developing countries as printed in a special U.N. document about the inter-connection between social progress and the population increase (E/3895, dated November 24, 1964).

"Industrial, agricultural, and cultural progress has enabled the Soviet Union to liquidate the evil inheritance of the tsarist regime and the war-caused chaos. By 1964, the national income of the U.S.S.R. rose 23-fold in comparison with the level of 1913, and 21-fold in relation to every citizen of the country. Mass urbanization, the increase of the general cultural level, the involvement of women in productive activity: all this has combined to decrease the population growth rate to less than half. At the same time the natural population increase remains at a satisfactory level, but is topped several times by the economic development which in 1966–67 showed a 7.2 percent annual gross national product increase.

"And if in the developing countries the increased birthrate is causing temporary difficulties, the solution of the problem lies in the development of economy and culture."

Then Podyachikh comes out with a blanket assertion: "Not in a single country in the world has birth control produced positive results. The solution of the problem lies only in radical socio-economic changes."

However, G. Gerasimov, the political commentator of Novosti Press Agency in Moscow expanded on this: "Demographers have calculated that to support an annual population increase of 1 percent, a society must annually expand its gross national product by 4 percent. If a country reaches the high annual national product growth of 8 percent, the increase in population of 2 percent will liquidate the benefits of such economic increase. And the demographic speedometer of the world is hovering around 2 percent.

"No doubt at all: Social, economic, and cultural development is the main weapon against a population explosion. But, one should add to it the necessity of supplementary measures known as demographic policies.

"In the Soviet Union the question of having or not having children is decided by the family, and not at government level. The government role is limited to the help given to mothers of numerous children, and to the imposition of the bachelor tax. This is a birthrate stimulation policy. But at the same time, abortions are legal and free, and contraceptives are available. So the state is ready to help any Soviet family to make its choice."

Considering specifically demographic problems facing the Soviet Union *Nauka i zhizn* (*Science and Life*) in 1969 conducted a special interview with Professor Boris Urlanis, who is considered to be the foremost demographic expert of the Soviet Union.

"Question: How does the Soviet Union stand in the matter of birthrate?

"Answer: The birthrate in the Soviet Union has considerably decreased during the last five years. In 1963 we had 212 births for every 10,000 of the population, and in 1967— only 174. And this index varies greatly throughout the country. For instance, in Azerbaidjan in 1967 it stood at 324, in Turkmenia at 356, but in the Russian Federation, the Ukraine, Esthonia, Latvia and Lithuania the figure was very much lower. The lowest birthrate is in Moscow, Leningrad, Kiev, Kharkov and other large cities.

"Question: At the turn of the century the birthrate in rural areas was considerably higher than in urban centers. How is this situation today?

"Answer: The birthrate in the country is still higher than that in cities, but the difference is not as great as it was once —not over 25%. But while in 1913 some 82% of the population lived in rural regions, today more than half lives in urban communities, and the urbanization process will continue.

"Question: Do biological factors play an important part?

"Answer: No, with the exception of hereditary sterility of some women. A more important factor is the age structure of mothers. The high birthrate in pre-Revolutionary Russia was explained, for instance, by the fact that most women married while very young. In 1910, over half of all brides were below

the age of twenty. The way this situation has changed during
the last fifty years can be gleaned from the following table:

Age of bride	Percent in 1910	Percent in 1960
Under 20	54.5	26.0
21–25	31.0	40.7
26–30	7.3	11.6
31–40	4.7	10.9
41–50	1.9	4.2
Over 50	0.6	6.3

"Question: Is it possible to regulate the birthrate?

"Answer: In our time the birthrate in one great nation
has decreased to less than half, and this has led to the stabiliza-
tion of the population index. I speak of Japan which in all
probability will never have a population of over 100 million.
The government of India is planning to cut the birthrate of
the country by half in the future.

"In France, where the low birthrate was proverbial, this
situation has been largely corrected by the demographic policies of the state. I mean, the financial support of large families. The same policies have been introduced in Hungary, Bul-
garia, Jugoslavia and some other countries.

"This proves that the birthrate can be influenced, and
therefore, can be planned.

"Question: At what stage of married life should married
couples have children?

"Answer: Medicine tells us that the healthiest children
are born to young mothers, to women below the age of thirty.

"Question: How many children, in your opinion, should
every couple have?

"Answer: From the standpoint of the state it is necessary
that each Soviet family have two or three children. For the

mere maintenance of the population at the present level ten
married couples must have a total of twenty-three children.

"Question: Does it mean that in the Soviet Union we
must take definite measures for increasing the birthrate?

"Answer: I believe that in the republics with a low birthrate the government must introduce family encouragement
measures in the form of cash subsidies for the second and third
child, since the appearance of the first child usually does not
depend on material considerations. I believe that such changes
in our demographic policies would stimulate the birthrate in
those regions where it has decreased."

The idea of cash payments for children is not new even
in the Soviet Union where it is now practised in some very
small measure. But it evokes resentment among many women.
One said that this method would equate women with sows
on a pig farm. Any idea of being forced into motherhood is
vaguely insulting to the emancipated Soviet woman—at least
to those in the higher educational and cultural levels.

Although complete freedom from all material considerations was a basic principle of the Revolution, economics play
a very important part in the lives of the Soviet people. And
interest in such matters has been growing with the general
rise of prosperity. And, in fact, in those places where the general level of prosperity reaches a sufficiently high level and
where housing conditions are good, the birthrate has been increasing.

Bratsk in Siberia holds the national birthrate record; and
here workers are paid hardship bonuses which almost double
wages in comparison with those in the central parts of the
country. Another example is the metallurgical city Norilsk,
lying above the Arctic Circle in Siberia. Here, out of a population of 155,000, over 50,000 are children. The explanation

is not that the Arctic night lasts for over four months each year, as some cynics say, but because workers are paid very high wages, and have more amenities of life than in most parts of the country. There is a very definite connection between the still rather low standard of living in the Soviet Union and married couples' resistance against having large families.

V. Perevedentsev, already quoted on divorces, frankly admits this. In his article "How Many Children?" published in *Literaturnaya Gazetta* in 1969, he comes out strongly for some government action on a purely economic level to stimulate the birthrate.

"In the not so distant past, children were looked upon by parents as an insurance for a secure old age. They were regarded as future *providers*. This function of children is decreasing rapidly. For the vast majority of the aged, pensions have become the main source of income, rather than the material assistance of their children.

"At the same time, the expense of raising children has increased despite the help of the state (in the form of crèches, kindergartens, schools, medical expenses, etc.) Only forty years ago 80 percent of the population of the Soviet Union lived in rural areas, but now the majority lives in urban centers. If in rural districts boys of ten to twelve became valuable helpers, children now remain basically only consumers until they are twenty. The expenses for raising children were once considered as a form of loan to be repaid to parents during their old age. But now such a loan has not only increased in size, but has become not repayable. The interest, and a very large interest, is received by the society as a whole.

"Of course the question of family planning rests on many considerations, but the economic one should not be dismissed. The cost of bringing up children has increased, and the fruits are collected primarily by the society. Therefore it would be only just that the society take upon itself a larger share of such cost. The raising of children requires much labor, and hard labor at that. The weight of this labor falls mostly upon women. A working mother has in effect a double load: eight hours at work, plus five to six hours at home.

"By raising children women produce the foremost necessity of the society—people who then create all the material and spiritual values. And this most important labor is probably the only form of any socially valuable labor which remains unpaid for. The fact is that families with many children inevitably find themselves at an economic disadvantage in comparison with small families.

"In the Soviet Union the state renders financial help to parents. But even though this involves as a whole tremendous sums, the individual payments are much too insignificant to stimulate the birthrate. For each third child the couple received 20 rubles at birth; for the fourth—65 rubles at birth and 4 rubles each month during the first four years; for the fifth—85 and 6 rubles respectively; for the sixth—100, and 7 rubles; for the seventh and eighth—125 and 10 rubles; for the ninth and tenth—175 and 12.5 rubles; for the eleventh and each subsequent child—250 and 15 rubles.

"But the greatest economic difficulties often follow the birth of the *first* child. Let us take a hypothetic case. Both young parents earn 100 rubles per month. While they are alone, this is sufficient. Now there appears a child. Mother, at the end of her paid-for leave, often has to leave her work for a while. Now there are 100 rubles for three. So it may often happen that young parents, remembering this period, avoid the repetition of this experience.

"Since the fruits of children's upbringing are reaped mostly by society, society must pay for this work as for any other socially useful work under socialism, *in accordance with its quantity and quality.*

"This would require enormous sums. So where shall we get them? Some people suggest lowering the general wage

level and using the resulting economy for the support of families with many children. I consider this, just as the increased
tax on childless men, unrealistic.

"The following appears to me to be more rational. The
tempo of pay increases could be slowed up, and the resulting
saved sums could be plowed back into the general prosperity
in the form of a *gradually increasing* (along with the increasing national income) *subsidies for children.* And, for several
years to come such payments should be limited *only for families in lower income brackets.*

"We should note that the rise of the standard of living
through increased wages started only after 1953. Before then
it was affected by the decrease of consumer goods prices.

"Decreased consumer goods prices, increased wages and
salaries, and payments for children, are all different methods
of increasing the general national income of people. But, naturally, different methods affect different segments of people.
The main beneficiaries would be couples with several children. And the losers would be the childless couples and those
with a single child.

"The demographic value of this measure would lie in the
fact that if childbirth ceased to affect the standard of living,
the economic reasons for limiting childbirth would be eliminated.

"The important question is—who should get paid? Most
demographers consider that these payments should augment
the salaries and wages of male heads of families. I consider
this wrong. Shall we reestablish the economic dependence of
women? The one who spends most of her time raising children should receive these payments. In the majority of cases
those are mothers. These payments should be wages paid for
this work.

"I believe that such payments would permit us to reestablish the *normal* level of birthrate.

"Of course, we must consider other factors as well. One

of them would be the decrease of the number of women engaged in the nation's economy. Can the society afford it? First let us look at the principle. The involvement of women in the national economy was a very progressive measure. I am convinced that woman must work, but not at all stages of her life.

"I think that the rational situation for woman would be to work until the birth of her first child, and after the last one has been raised. The size of this gap would depend largely on the level of child-care help woman gets from the state, a level which leaves much to be desired at present.

"Now let us take a practical view. What would happen if several million women should leave the national economy? There is much talk lately about the so-called shortage of labor in the country. As a specialist, I consider these views to be incorrect. I will name now three sources of additional labor.

"First, industry. Many industrial enterprises are overstaffed. Specialists estimate that this overstaffing reaches twenty to thirty percent in some places. These enterprises can release enough labor for others who need it.

"Secondly, agriculture. Some 30 percent of our labor force is engaged in this sector, while in many countries five to ten percent supply all the needs of their societies.

"The third source is pensioners. A large number of them can be prevailed upon to return to productive work.

"I am convinced that labor reserves of the country are large enough to permit the release of women while they are engaged in raising children. And during all the time they are so engaged they should be paid *wages,* and this time should be computed against their retirement pensions. This would be another step towards giving these women economic equality with their husbands."

The editors were flooded with letters from woman readers almost universally protesting against these suggestions. Perevedetsev was accused of male chauvinism, and his suggestions were branded as a vicious attempt to push women back into nurseries and kitchen.

The official attitude of the ruling Communist party can be gleaned from the address delivered at the World Women's Congress in Helsinki on June 15, 1969, by the high priestess of Soviet women's lib, Valentina Tereshkova-Nikolaeva, the first and the only woman cosmonaut in the world. It is important to remember that she is not only the president of the Soviet Women's Committee, but a member of the predominantly male Central Committee of the Communist party.

She came out strongly for woman's right to participate fully in the economic life in all societies as the only way for women to achieve liberation. Soviet women, she said, would never retreat from the position which they have won. According to her, the survey conducted in the Soviet Union disclosed that 30 percent of the working women there considered moral reasons the most important factor in their careers, but all cited it as a secondary reason, after economic necessity.

She came out sharply against any and all attempts to curtail women's economic opportunities in order to allow them to have more time for taking care of their children and homes.

"Some modern scientists," she declared, "underline the incompatibility of woman's functions in those two spheres, suggest returning to the old traditional division of labor between the sexes. Men, according to them, should work and support their families, and women should be wives, mothers, and keepers of homes. This attitude is absolutely contrary to all present realities. The full participation of women in economic activities is an irreversible process.

"Others, realizing this fact, suggest lightening the overall load of woman. However, they want to achieve this not by social government measures, designed to improve the general conditions of woman's life, but by limiting her professional activities.

"Some suggest that mothers of small children should take a break in their careers until their children have sufficiently grown up. According to them, woman's life should be divided into three periods: getting an education, bearing and raising her children, and then starting to work, after the children have sufficiently grown up, at the age of thirty-five to forty. They support this by the assertion that women live longer than men, and that their retirement age can be extended to sixty-five.

"Life does not fit this scheme. It would create a number of problems. The most important one would be the professional standing of such women. Science and technology develops so swiftly that any working person must constantly improve his qualifications. If a woman disconnects herself from her profession for fifteen to twenty years, it would be impossible for her to regain her original qualifications. She would be only able to work as an unqualified laborer, in jobs which are poorly paid and are difficult to get. Statistics show that among all the unemployed women in the world more than half are in the thirty-plus age group.

"Some sociologists advocate the shortening of woman's working week. They feel that this would eradicate the present contradictions between her professional and domestic functions. Working part time, woman would not be disconnected from her profession while being able to contribute something to the family's income, and devote enough time to raising her children.

"But such part-time workers cannot count on any solid professional careers, and would be used mostly as supplementary and temporary labor."

According to Tereshkova-Nikolaeva the solution lies in the further development of child-care facilities as well as communal dining rooms, family clubs, etc. What needs adjusting is not the professional part of woman's life, but the part spent at home: the maximum release of the working woman from unproductive domestic activities.

One must agree with this. In fact, in accordance with early theories of Marx and Engels, the entire task of raising children should be eventually taken over by the state. Seemingly an ideal solution but how would this square up with the biological urge of woman not only to bear children but take care of them and to raise them? And again—doesn't this conflict with the avowed aim of the Soviet state to strengthen the family?

In this light, it is interesting to quote another Soviet woman, a young doctor and a mother of two children: Intelligent and enthusiastic, she has an independent mind, and is not reluctant to speak it in a vigorous and uncompromising way during a private discussion.

"The only fault with everything so far proposed for women in our country," she told me, "is that the proposals came from men. I know that as a good Marxist I should not disconnect woman's problem from general social problems, and that true woman's liberation comes only with the liberation of the entire human race from old social and economic oppressions. With communism.

"Still, I am a woman and you are a man. You can advance the most marvelous theories, but I will eventually have to bear my children in agony and in anguish. Socialism can't change this fact. And no man can feel what a mother feels— or can even imagine her feelings.

"Sex is not a popular subject with us. We have been shying from it like ostriches burying their heads in the sand. But, ostriches do not bury their heads, and secondly, sex is still a tremendously important part of every person's physiological makeup. It is more important for woman than man because of the consequences that stay with her after the sex act has been completed. Unfortunately sex is often confused with lust—and it is in this department that men are more endowed than women.

"Why do I say this? Only because we have been limiting all discussions of woman's part in the modern world to economics and sociology—and have been overlooking the sexual part of the problem. The traditional sex attitudes which have been designed by men from the dawn of time should be re-designed in the light of the new position of woman not only in our country—but throughout the world.

"It is all very well to discuss and calculate how many children every woman must have to maintain the demographic balance. But what all those planners overlook is that with the economic changes there have come some changes in the sphere of woman's personal life. Economic pressures may influence her decisions for a while, but that is not a radical solution, just a temporary one. Woman will stop bearing children just as soon as her urge to have them is satisfied, and from there on nothing but her own decision will make her continue her procreative activities.

"With economic independence comes sex independence. Some emergency economic measures can slow down this process, but they cannot stop or reverse it. And if the pressures to reverse it grow, this may lead to a spontaneous Lysistrata-like resistance of women.

"This may sound frivolous but it isn't. In my work I speak to thousands of young women applying for abortions. Very many of them do this because of economic reasons; but there are quite a few who do it because they have been pressured by men responsible for their conditions to have children. They are subconsciously insulted by such pressures, often even without realizing it themselves. In fact, women's consultation clinics are better places to study demographic problems than demographers' offices.

"No, I don't subscribe to the idea that life is a battle

between sexes. This is stupid because women enjoy sex just as much as men; they like to be loved, but they also like to love. They are physiologically attracted to men, just as much as men are to them. The sexes need one another. Their interests are common. Anything which hurts women, hurts men even more; men are losers every time women are dissatisfied or oppressed. It was Engels who said that first.

"What I mean is that no decision about economic or social measures involving women should be taken without the widest participation of women in the decision. I say this not because of any female chauvinism, but simply because such decisions taken without women will not work in the long run in the modern era. One must remember that from no other field has woman been excluded so long and so consistently as in the sphere of her sex activities. Religions, traditions, customs, governments, scientists, and men in general have been telling her how she should feel about sex, when to enjoy and not enjoy it, when and where to have children, how many, and how to take care of them and how to raise them. Her emotional and physiological freedom has been violated even more than her body for countless centuries; and this cannot and will not continue. All social and political changes inevitably entail changes in sex attitudes. This is natural, and this is healthy; but unfortunately few people are willing to face this reality. They want to force woman back into old attitudes, every time she dares to venture out.

"Why do I dwell so much on sex? Only because this part of the problem has been consistently overlooked—it has been considered man's domain. Sex may not be as important to woman as it is to man; but without this part, all other parts just don't fit together. Modern woman, who has learned to pay her own way through life, will not be kept out of any part of it.

"Only frank and open discussion of all areas of the so-called woman problem—including sex—and woman's active participation in shaping all legislation concerning marriage, family, children, and yes, sex—in and out of marriage—can lead to correct solutions, can save the family as we know it. Since woman must bear the most difficult, painful, and lasting part of the family relationship, it is woman who must participate in all decisions about all family matters, on all levels. No laws, even those designed to help her, will work unless they are designed with her participation. Given a chance to do so, modern, educated and independent woman will find ways to adjust the contradictions in her present position, and to perform her biological functions conscientiously, efficiently, and responsibly. What she will not accept, are decisions made *for* her by sociologists, economists, demographers, and politicians."

I was impressed. Such an intelligent and courageous woman! But when I asked her whether I could quote her in my book, there came a cop out. She preferred that I not use her name. "My name means nothing but some people might misunderstand, particularly if this is published abroad."

Dilbar Abdurakhmanova, an Uzbek, is the orchestra leader at the Tashkent Theatre of Opera and Ballet. Once Uzbek women led harem lives.

9. Sex and the Soviet Girl

Sex, like everything else in the Soviet Union, had its ideological ups and downs.

The Revolution brought a wave of sex permissiveness in its wake . . . when bourgeois sentimentality and romanticism were sneered at. Sex was treated physiologically, "without lilacs,"—a mutually pleasurable physical exercise with no loose ends. For the first time woman was accepted as an equal partner in this—and not a mere commodity for man. Many girls flaunted their promiscuity as a sign of their liberation from religious and traditional taboos.

Then during the first industrialization years, came the era of Orwellian puritanism. Girls were supposed to lavish their libido on tractors and bridges, and engage in sex only if and when they had free time for it. Boys were supposed to be fired up by political enthusiasm to the point of virtual sexlessness. Marriage became a contract of two conscientious workers rather than bedmates. Presumably two could study Marx better than one. Ideological affinity was considered the paramount requisite for marriage with periodic sex as a way of keeping bodies in shape for work. It was good for mental health—insured productive stability. Love was a mutual attraction of two true comrades sharing common enthusiasm for the tremendous task of building the socialist society.

Romanticism came back during the war years. The female image has been a powerful emotional weapon sustaining warriors from earliest prehistory. Food and women were the two basic needs of primitive man; he had to fight for both. In early days of human history women were included among the spoils of war. Moses, the earliest spokesman for God, thus commanded the warriors of Israel returning from war and bringing women and children as spoils of victory: "Have you let all the women live? . . . Kill every male among the little ones, and every woman who has known man by lying with him. But all the young girls who have not known man by lying with him, keep alive for yourselves." *

Sex and war mixed well in more recent times as well. Many celebrated songs of the last few wars had a woman image as their theme: "Madeleine," "Lili Marlene," "Mary from Tipperary," and even the proverbial "Mademoiselle from Armentier." The most popular song among the Soviet soldiers during the last war was about the lovely "Katusha" pining for her faraway beloved, and carefully saving her love for his return.

In wartime the woman image always had two facets: a staunchly faithful girl waiting for soldier at home, and a readily available beauty to comfort soldier between battles.

After the war, when the repopulation of the country became an all-important problem in the Soviet Union, the mother image became paramount. Woman the producer of children, the Soviet madonna and child, intensely moral despite her often husbandless status. She was beautiful, tender, intensely desirable, yet pure—motherhood for her was not so much a product of sex as the fulfillment of her highest ideals.

But sex, of course, could not be excluded altogether. Gradually—after Stalin's death—it became a mentionable subject, and in very recent years love has become a respectable word, not without a sexual connotation when it involves man and woman. Even such once-despised conceptions as romanticism and chivalry are very much back in the official

---

* Num. 31:16–17

Soviet parlance. "With us man's chivalry is very much valued," Mrs. Shibarina of the Soviet Women's Committee told me. "It is a very desirable quality of a true man of high Soviet culture."

Tempora mutantur . . .

Sex is one sphere of human activity which has never been accurately prescribed by Communist theoreticians. However, in a true communist society sex would lose its connection with economics: it would cease to be a commodity to be sold or bought, in marriage or out of it. No man would be able to buy sex since money and all other symbols of personal wealth would disappear, and no woman would be able to sell her body for the same reason, nor forced to withhold it from any man she loves and who loves her. Marriage would cease to be a legal contract, but would become a free union of two people who chose to have mutual relations. All such unions would be freely dissolvable just as soon as one of the parties wishes to terminate it.

Children? Again economic considerations would play no part here. The society would be in full charge of their support and education with no economic responsibilities attached to parenthood.

Theoretically, this would eliminate all the unhappiness created in the present society by dependence of one person on another. But this presupposes not merely a complete liberation of woman, but her absolute economic and emotional equality with man. All vestiges of a double standard applicable to the sexes would disappear completely becoming only a vague memory of "capitalist barbarism" which once existed.

But what about love? Jealousy? Biological and physiological possessiveness? Unrequited affection? Disparity of sex urges? Sexual deviations? And a whole host of other problems not connected with economics?

Marxism seems to have no answers to those questions. Hopefully, in an ideal communist society many of those things would naturally adjust themselves with the minimum of interference from society.

But no one, not even the most ardent Communist, would claim that such an ideal society has been achieved in the Soviet Union. He would only claim that socialism, as practiced there, will eventually create the basis for communism, in some more or less remote future. Until such a happy situation is achieved, society must exercise some legal regimentation in all spheres of human activities, including sex.

Marriage is taken very seriously in the Soviet Union today—with some very definite economic responsibilities involved in it. The only way in which it differs from marriage in capitalist society is the more or less enforced economic independence of woman on the basic level—the termination of marriage entails no economic hardship on the woman's part. Even if she earns a low income, as many women do, it is enough to take care of her basic needs.

There is still another side: marriage, as a rule, does not offer any degree of economic security for woman, or any noticeable improvement in her standard of living. There are exceptions, of course. Obviously the wife of a high-placed functionary, specialist, scientist, or artist lives better than a wife of a truck driver or a factory worker, even if in both situations she continues to work herself. So economics still play some part in marital relations—though to a lesser degree than in most Western societies.

That covers marriage. But Soviet women as a rule, do not marry young; and men often wait even longer. What do they do about sex meanwhile?

There is no accurate answer for the whole country. Regional customs vary greatly from one part of the country to another, from urban communities to villages, from large cities to small ones, and much depends on the educational level in each of those cases.

There are no statistics about sex activities of Soviet citizens. The official Party attitude is that sex is a private matter for each man and woman—and that it must be kept private. Though sexology is not recognized as a science, this does not mean that sex subjects are not studied by physicians, educators, sociologists, psychologists, and legislators. They are. Sex information is available to anyone honestly seeking it. What is not generally available is public display of it in the form of popular books, magazines, sexy shows, or films. Sex is not treated as merchandise.

This creates an impression of official puritanism. Especially pornography is considered to be a crime, or rather its commercial dissemination is. But pornography is notoriously difficult to define accurately. Courts in many countries have struggled with this problem with no final answer. When I asked a well-known scientist in Moscow to define pornography for me, he answered, "Anything which might attract the abnormal attention of a child."

This question was answered in more detail by a famous Soviet writer who often traveled abroad and was familiar with the present trends towards complete elimination of all restrictions concerning obscenity and pornography. "The arguments offered by advocates of freedom of speech and artistic expression in all sex matters are basically dishonest because what they defend is not a principle, but their right to produce and sell pornography for their own profit—without considering any possible harm it may do to others. It would be interesting to see what would happen if along with a complete freedom to produce pornography, there would have been a law making all profits derived from pornography illegal. How many of those freedom militants would remain in business for purely idealistic motives? Probably very few. The fact is that writers, artists, and publishers producing pornography are moved by the profit motive; and in the vast majority of cases, by absolutely nothing else. Some also want to create publicity—to attract attention to themselves, again to cash in on this.

"I have followed several court actions concerning pornography in America and England, and usually no medical advice was involved, no child psychologists or educators consulted. Only the so-called experts to determine if any considered work was art or not. But the term *art* is even less definable than *obscenity*.

"I am not speaking about sex education—that is different. Any village child watching animals knows that copulation is natural and normal, and he usually knows that his parents engage in it. That does not hurt him, and does not give him any lopsided idea about human values. And as often as not he is not particularly interested in that facet of life, no more than he is interested in other organic functions of human body. But no one charges him money for letting him watch two copulating dogs—or human beings—thus perverting his sense of values.

"Every freedom has its limits. Freedom of speech does not mean that a man can yell *fire!* in a crowded theatre to cause a stampede and hurt people. Here the law protects the interests of the public by constraining one person's freedom. It is a duty of every government to protect those who might be hurt, by activities of any one individual or a group of individuals. One cannot sell hashish on the basis of the freedom of commerce. All laws restrict individual freedom in some degree. When we do not permit dissemination of pornography, or even a suggestive work of art pandering to prurient interests and instincts, we are protecting the society, and particularly children and young people because the consensus of scientific opinion holds such dissemination harmful to them.

"Please note that in Russia we have no legal restriction on any sex activities for as long as they are conducted in private. Such restrictions are impossible to enforce anyway. Whenever they exist, they are used mostly for blackmail and mostly by women demanding divorce and alimony. 'He forced me into perversion—I couldn't stand it.' "

"But wouldn't a wife in Russia get a divorce on such grounds?" I asked.

"Undoubtedly, but not a single kopeck. This is the whole point. We don't permit commercial exhibition or exploitation of sex. One can write pornography, but not publish or sell it. One can engage in any sex practices with willing partners, but not do it in public or charge money for it. You will say that there are still girls in Moscow who would sleep with foreign tourists for foreign money. Of course. Undoubtedly there is also underground pornography produced, circulated, and sold. But it is one thing to have such things, and another to legalize them because they exist. Then why not legalize murder and theft because they occur, and no law in history could eliminate them?

"There are such things as public decency and social hygiene. Even in Sweden and Denmark they don't permit people to copulate in parks, or urinate on street corners. That has nothing to do with puritanism. Much of your pornography is produced for the sake of scandal, and all of it for the sake of profit—none for artistic motives. Would Venus of Milo become more artistic if you paste some pubic hair on her? But that would certainly make money—you would have people queueing up to look at her. And that is just what many of your writers, artists, and publishers do—because they can't sell their stuff otherwise, they put pubic hair on it.

"I read somewhere that your president was appalled by pornography in America, but had no legal way to stop it. I can give him advice. Let him order his tax people to pay

particular attention to smut producers and peddlers. If they
could stop Al Capone, they could stop many of those freedom
militants as well."

This might be practical advice. Generally, Russians cannot understand why any government might be helpless to do
anything because of absence of laws, or loopholes in laws.
"If it is in the interests of the majority of the people, isn't it
undemocratic not to do it?" is the usual argument. This is not
a Soviet phenomenon, but reflects the historical Russian dis-
trust of legal technicalities. "Laws are like the traces of a
carriage," according to the old Russian proverb. "They turn
any way the horse turns."

For a casual traveler, particularly if he does not speak
the language, the Soviet Union would appear as a practically
sexless society. No sexy displays, not on magazine or book
covers, nor in ads, and not even on calendars. No courting
couples locked in passionate embrace on park benches or
lawns. Even simple kissing in public is unusual. Lovers
customarily consider holding hands as the maximum display
of affection in public.

All this is misleading. Extreme modesty in public behavior has been a tradition in Russia for centuries, particularly among women. Until very recently anything pertaining
to sex was not a subject to be discussed if women were present—even veiled allusions and innuendos would cause em-
barrassment. This has changed, but does not approach the
extent of loose sex talk which one often hears among young-
sters of both sexes in permissive Western societies. One still
has to choose words. Four-letter words (and all of them have
more than four letters in Russia) are still confined only to
masculine company, even though occasional slips of the
tongue do occur.

Russian men are extremely fond of using obscenity while
talking among themselves. This sort of verbal roughness be-

came an affectation among men after the Revolution, even among intellectuals. In early postrevolutionary years, proving one's proletarian origin was all important—any sort of refinement was suspect. Conditions have changed, but the affectation is still there. And it has even assumed a certain aura of smartness. I was once present during a business conference, involving only men, when a highly sophisticated firm executive wanted to make the point that the deal under discussion was an experiment. The way he expressed this could be rendered into English as follows: "Don't forget, Comrades, that we are fucking a virgin here." No one was taken aback; and the rejoinder was: "Not quite—they did this at Mosfilm last year."

This could never occur if a woman was present. This trend expressed by a Russian term *muzhichestvovat* (emulating peasants) have never involved women. On the contrary, while peasant women and girls were quite used to men using blue expressions in their presence, this has been considered extremely uncultured ever since the Revolution. A few sophisticated ladies will occasionally slip in a profanity for the sake of being chic, but an average Soviet woman's speech is free from it. The average woman will no longer pretend that she does not understand rough anatomical words, as Russian women did once; but she does not encourage profanity in her presence. Men usually watch their language when speaking to women, often becoming almost tongue-tied due to their everyday habit of using four-letter words.

If changing sex-behavior patterns have been seriously studied in the Soviet Union, the information is not readily available. One must depend on personal observations, and occasional frank discussions with knowledgeable men: women would rarely discuss sex with strangers.

The general impression is that sex *mores* have certainly changed since the patriarchal prerevolutionary days, or even since the days of the Stalinist enforced puritanism. These changes particularly affected women, and even more so young girls, because men enjoyed considered sex freedom even under patriarchal customs. So these changes should be considered a part of the general emancipation of women.

Among smaller nationalities and ethnic groups, some ancient tribal customs still survive. But even they are dying out for the simple reason that young people usually leave their ancestral habitats and move into urban centers. Occasionally in the high reaches of the Caucasus, for instance, a young husband may still deliver his bride to her parents and seek divorce because the girl has proved to lack the Biblical token of virginity, but those occasions are very rare, and are related now as anecdotes proving the backwardness of the people involved.

In urban centers it is generally assumed that any unmarried girl has a perfect right to engage in sex activities and no young bride is expected to be a virgin in the medical *virgo intacta* sense. The word *virginity* seems to have lost its meaning in this sense. I have spoken to young men who did not even know that a hymen was a natural part of female anatomy. And I have been told on good medical authority that many young girls intentionally destroyed this obstacle by the simple use of their fingers, or sought surgical help to eliminate it. A Russian doctor told me that a girl of eighteen once came to her with such a request motivating her plea by the fact that she was about to be married, and did not want her husband to know that she had never engaged in intercourse before.

This may be an extreme case, but it is no longer *à la mode* for young woman to play the shrinking violet. Although sex education is not included in the curriculum of Soviet schools, any girl of fifteen, or even younger, can get necessary medical information from the numerous women's clinics. If she is too bashful, some of her less retiring girl friends would supply her with information from the clinics.

Oddly enough, boys seem to be more ignorant in sex matters than girls since there are no special men's clinics. They still have to depend on secondhand information which they pick up from more experienced boys. There is also a matter of pride: traditionally boys are supposed to know everything, while girls do not hesitate to seek information as a part of their newly liberated status.

How widespread is promiscuity among young Russians? "They are copulating like flies," a knowledgeable Russian writer once told me. I am sure that this is an exaggeration, but I was told about a girl of seventeen from a good family who had had nine abortions, and was quite willing to discuss this. Even considering the general sexual liberation of Soviet women, for a seventeen-year-old girl to have nine abortions is certainly unusual and atypical, and probably should be attributed to the girl's bravado.

It is almost impossible to generalize about the sex habits of Soviet young people because of the wide diversity of local customs and ethnic backgrounds. In large industrial communities where thousands of young people live and work together and in education centers which are always coeducational, habits are vastly different from small rural areas where everyone knows everyone, and where parental supervision is stricter and more immediate.

The general impression is that sex as it is practiced in urban centers of the Soviet Union does not have the morbid and prurient connotation it often has in Western societies. Above everything else, it is accepted and treated as a perfectly normal physiological function. This is probably explained by the basic peasant roots of the majority of modern Soviet youth; peasants take sex for granted. Animal breeding is part of their occupation. The absence of literature or films designed to appeal to prurient tastes undoubtedly also plays a considerable part in this situation.

Copulation among the young is usually just that. Oral

stimulation, known locally as French love is restricted to more sophisticated men and women. Cunnilingus is practiced among them, and is often discussed among men, who often consider it a perfectly normal activity since many animals practice it before intercourse. Fellatio, however, seems to be very rare, and practiced only by experienced seductresses of the highest sex sophistication, but is eagerly sought by experienced men. Oral ejaculation seems to be rigidly avoided— even by the most sensuous women.

Since there are no such organizations like the Kinsey institute or the Masters research center, there is no factual information about the prevalence of such practices, and percentages can only be estimated. It is a safe guess, however, that they are considerably lower than in modern Western societies. Perhaps 10 percent of the couples in cities practice occasional cunnilingus, and less than 5 percent of the women have practiced fellatio even once during their lifetimes. Even these percentages may be high.

A foreigner residing in Moscow for many years and known for his sexual prowess complained to me about the general lack of intimate personal hygiene among Soviet women. This well may be so since no sex hygiene aids are ever advertised or available in general commerce.

The only readily available contraceptives are condoms for men. The so-called pill has not yet been released for general use since some clinical tests are still continuing. Protracted tests, often lasting for many years, are required before any medication is released. The method generally recommended to married women desiring to avoid pregnancies is an intrauterine device, inserted into the womb by a qualified medical specialist. Few young unmarried girls avail themselves of this convenience, which is available only through women's clinics. Since condoms are generally disliked by men—and some women who claim they interfere with the feeling of intimacy during intercourse, abortion is still by far the most popular method of getting rid of any unwanted complications of sex relations.

Medical authorities insist that the venereal disease rate is much lower in the Soviet Union than in other European countries, citing the absence of prostitution as the main reason. Also some prophylactic measures are widely recommended to all young men; they are available free of charge and in some situations are even enforced. During military service all men returning from leaves must pass a medical examination and preventive treatment. No stigma is attached to this, and much is being done by medical personnel to combat the feeling of false shame. This is particularly important since the overwhelming majority of all practicing physicians are women. But men are treated by men and women by women in cases of venereal disease or sex prophylaxis, unless no doctor of the desired sex is available—as often happens in small towns or villages.

The emancipation of women has produced a universal recognition of woman's right to enjoy sex, in and out of marriage, on an equal basis with men. While in old Russia no decent woman would ever admit that she derived pleasure in intercourse for fear of being considered a tart, young Soviet women today not only freely admit it, but demand it as a right. One hears constant complaints from men about Soviet women becoming very choosy, uppity, and demanding in sex relations; and every man who wishes his marriage or affair to last must be very adroit sexually.

One hears about sex orgies supposedly taking place in large Soviet cities; but that is undoubtedly an exaggeration. The idea of group sex has not as yet hit Russia. Soviet girls are still quite outwardly modest by Western standards.

Of course the shortage of housing plays weird tricks in the realm of human relations. All living and loving space is at a premium, and young people must be ingenious in finding it for their sex activities. I, personally, knew a lady in Moscow who supplemented her meager pension by letting her friends use her room occasionally as a clandestine love nest. Illegal as this is, it is not an uncommon practice. Frequently parents intentionally go out to provide the opportunity for their sons and daughters to entertain their sweethearts, or couples might take turns in private quarters during parties; but these things cannot be equated to orgies in the Western sense. Sex is still practiced very much in private in Russia.

It has been also suggested that sexual looseness among the young people has a protest character: life is dull and drab, and sex is the only area in which the ever-present government does not meddle. This might be partly true since sex provides a welcome release from constant civic supervision. In the case of young girls, particularly students, this is also a way to assert their liberation from parental restrictions and their equality with the boys—but again no Soviet girl need ever engage in any sex activities for any reason besides her own free choice. Economic considerations almost never play any part in sex relations between young people because young boys rarely have any money to lavish on their sweethearts, and no such attractions as swanky cars or flashy clothes.

Very rarely does one hear about sex deviations in Russia. Homosexuality is not generally recognized as a problem. Most girls and boys consider this an oriental vice. It was once widely practiced in the Caucasus and Moslem areas of the country where it was based mostly on the local customs which prevented young girls from associating with or even speaking to men, and on the *kalym* (marriage price) which few young men could afford. In other words, homosexuality was treated as a temporary substitute for heterosexual activities. The same situation existed in closed boarding schools, barracks, and work camps where young men had no opportunity to meet girls. Such situations have disappeared and so has "enforced" homosexual behavior. When such behavior is still encountered, it is treated with humorous tolerance rather than condemnation. It is generally considered to be an absolutely private affair. In fact it is extremely rarely encountered and generally not discussed outside of medical circles.

Before the Revolution, male homosexuality was wide spread among the upper classes in Russia. Such behavior was recognized and socially accepted even though it was a criminal offense in such civilized Western societies as England. A notorious case was that of the celebrated composer Tchaikovsky, whose attempted marriage ended in tragedy while his friends and admirers sympathized deeply with his predicament. The case of Oscar Wilde, whose work was very popular in Russia, shocked and bewildered his Russian admirers. The idea that a famous author could be sent to jail for having homosexual relations with willing partners was inconceivable, almost barbaric.

There have never been any legal restrictions on homosexuality in Russia; and there is none in Soviet laws as long as such behavior is conducted in private, does not outrage public decency, and does not involve children.

Female homosexuality is simply not recognized. In any event such behavior can be very easily disguised since very close and affectionate friendships among girls and women are an old tradition in Russia. Girls kiss and hug one another in public in a manner which would be considered slightly shocking in Western societies, and if any girl would declare that she adores Sonya or Natasha no one would suspect any abnormality.

Foreign visitors are often taken aback at the sight of men greeting each other with kisses; but once again this is an old Russian tradition which by no means indicates homosexual interest. This is a proper way to greet relatives or close friends, personal or even political. Anyone watching newsreels and telecasts emanating from Russia is familiar with the scenes of high Soviet functionaries greeting visiting foreign comrades with kisses. . . . not just embraces, but with honest to goodness mouth-to-mouth kisses.

Even though Russia has never been a permissive society in the Western sense, traditionally sex attitudes have been surprisingly tolerant in certain areas. There were frequent cases of incest, particularly in rural regions and particularly involving fathers-in-law and their daughters-in-law. There was a special term *snokhach* * describing such men. The Church condemned such practices; but unless a rape was involved, cases were rarely prosecuted by civil authorities. Wives of soldiers, known as *soldatka's,* were notorious for their loose behavior in old Russian villages; and small wonder. In the nineteenth century the term of military service was twenty-five years. Once drafted, men spent their lifetimes drilling and marching.

Rape, however, is a very serious criminal offense in the Soviet Union. Men are extremely careful in this respect, and Russian women know very well how to defend themselves from any unwanted attention. Generally women have the first and last say in all sex situations, including marriage; and any husband forcing his attentions on even an unwilling wife might be technically guilty of rape.

The modern tolerance of masturbation in Western Europe and America cuts no ice with Soviet parents, except perhaps those with some medical background. The practice among children is still generally considered harmful, and children are punished for it. But of course this does not stop it. There is a Russian saying that there are two categories

---

* The Russian word *snokha* means daughter-in-law.

of men; "Those who masturbate; and those who masturbate, but deny it."

Soviet sociologists boast that the Revolution has eliminated prostitution. This is not altogether correct. Any unattached foreign man visiting Russia will be approached by a girl, usually young, good looking, and speaking foreign languages. It would not take him long to discover that the purpose of such approach is no different than in any capitalist country. Sometimes the girl will suggest going to the man's room, or going to her place. If he inquires about the price for this service, he is usually told anything which he considers proper. Usually five American dollars or two English pounds suffices; and it must be a present and not a payment. It is not illegal to have sex, or accept presents, but accepting any payment for sex is a criminal offense. None of these charmers will accept Soviet rubles—no matter how many. This again is a technicality: a five-dollar bill is a souvenir, and so are two one-pound notes, but rubles cannot be explained away. (I have heard a story of one of these girls telling the police that she did not know that dollars were money. That sort of financial naïveté is curable, however—the girl got three years in a corrective labor camp.) There is a lively black market in foreign currency with the exchange rates many times higher than the official rate, and there are well-stocked stores where prices are very low, and unavailable luxury goods are on sale, which accept only foreign money.

Who are those girls, and where do they come from? Questioning them is senseless. They invariably say they are working or studying. They probably are, even if only as a cover.

It has often been suggested that all of them are secret police agents spying on foreigners. That could be logical perhaps in case of important foreign officials visiting the country, but not with respect to school teachers from Oklahoma or bookkeepers from Dulwich. The vast majority of foreign tourists represent no interest for the secret police.

"Just tramps," a Soviet journalist told me when I asked him about them. "The demoralized element seeking unearned money. Trash. Be careful about them—they often work for criminal blackmailers. We still have them here."

This may be so. But I have never heard of any foreigners getting into trouble because of them. There have been cases of foreign diplomats compromised by women working for the police; but first of all, those cases were extremely rare, and most of them occurred years ago. During Stalin's years when any contact with foreigners could mean dire trouble, there were young women known as *mozhno* girls who were permitted to associate with foreigners and report to the police (*mozhno* means, "it is permitted" in Russian). But it is difficult to believe that the secret police would employ scores of girls to spy on unimportant tourists. And yet, with the same girls working the same hotels, they must be known to hotel administration. There are even indications that they receive tips about single male foreigners staying in a given hotel. I have *never* been approached by them while traveling with my wife, and have *every* time when I was alone—sometimes by telephone. It should be remembered that there are no switchboards in Soviet hotels and every room has a separate line, so the information must be quite precise. In effect, they might be mozhno girls in some way accredited to tourist hotels.

I have been told that the girls never approach Soviet citizens staying at the same hotels despite the fact that some of those lonely men arriving in Moscow or Leningrad from the provinces might be desperately looking for such female companionship. But the girls zero in on only single male tourists, always foreigners.

The explanation probably lies with the generally relaxed police supervision, rising prosperity and some better quality consumer goods again available. Money, particularly foreign money, has become so valuable that the girls are willing to break the law and even pay for pertinent information out of their unearned income. It is also possible that some of them are connected with foreign currency speculators or even local police who close their eyes in exchange for small bribes for as long as the girls behave in a dignified manner and these girls invariably do. It has even been suggested that they are permitted to operate as a sort of tourist attraction, but this seems to be farfetched.

Nevertheless, lone foreign males are advised to proceed with caution, and always remember that while sleeping with a woman is no crime, paying for it is, and might lead to some pretty unpleasant consequences. Going to those girls' houses should be avoided—that can turn into a blackmail trap or they might be working for husky sweethearts who could fleece the victims.

Being an old married man I had no opportunity to investigate these charmers' proficiency, but some of my single and younger friends reported their complete satisfaction with what they got in exchange for their money. "Make no mistake," one of them said, "they are professionals of the highest order. There is nothing at all amateurish about them. They know what they are doing, and know how to do it."

The only way these girls differ from other Russian girls is that they are better dressed and misleadingly dignified and demure. Some of them are rare beauties, and all of them are very young and seemingly very well educated. The favorite haunts of the girls are bars, operated in conjunction with some tourist hotel, where only foreign currency is accepted.

Perhaps this is not be representative of all Russia. It is Moscow, and tourist Moscow at that. When I traveled in Siberia, there was no evidence of prostitution and my friends

there were very surprised when I recounted to them the scenes
I had observed in Moscow. "In some way this must be permitted," one of them said. "Our police is too efficient to be
fooled by those whores. Professional prostitution is just impossible to practice with us—and not because of morals, but
because of certain conditions of our society."

What are those conditions?

First of all, the Soviet Union is a goldfish-bowl society
with the minimum of unauthorized privacy permitted. The
most efficient check is housing. It is allocated by the government through trade unions, and only a person with proper
civic status can secure it. In addition, everyone must be
registered in a given locality, i.e. secure a residence permit
from the police. To secure the permit a person must have
proper employment, be studying, or have a family or relatives
willing to share their living space. Since working is an obligation of every able-bodied citizen, any non-working status
would become immediately suspect. Any private commercial
activity is considered to be speculation—a cardinal crime in
socialist society.

How would any woman wishing to engage in professional prostitution get around these obstacles?

Admittedly she could secure some cover employment,
perhaps on a part-time basis, and supplement her meager income by prostituting herself. But again she would have to
proceed with extreme caution since she can be at any time
denounced by her neighbors who invariably covet her living
space. She could invite men to her room, and even make love
to them; but if she started inviting many different men, others
would complain to the house delegate or the house committee
who administer all buildings. Perhaps she could get away with
it by bribing the delegate, but only for a little while.

In fact she would have to be devilishly inventive to practice prostitution on even a part-time basis since her income
may at any time be questioned by the authorities, and pro-

fessional prostitution is a criminal offense punishable with stiff terms of enforced labor. Also since the vast majority of Soviet men simply do not have enough money to make this trade worthwhile, overt prostitution, or prostitution as a profession, has been effectively stamped out; but not prostitution as a behavior. Any girl can have as many boyfriends as she wishes, and there is no law against her accepting presents, preferably not in the form of money, from them in exchange for her favors.

What has become absolutely impossible is enforced prostitution, as practiced in Western societies sometimes, when girls are kept in debt or find it impossible to earn their living in any other way. No Soviet girl can be forced into prostitution—that must be her free choice; and it can never become a permanent occupation. She must at all times have a source of provable earned income. The trick in Russia is not finding work, but avoiding it; and that is often almost impossible. But there are some exceptions. With rising prosperity many wives devote their time to domestic duties, being supported by their husbands. Today some 10 percent of able-bodied women can be classed as full-time housewives. This is not illegal; but such a status is not admired and entails some serious consequences. Some employment record is required to obtain pensions above the minimum of 45 rubles per month, and pensions are an all-important factor in present-day Russian economy. There might also be questions about the living space occupied by such nonworking wives.

Some girls might obtain a more or less fictional working status by declaring themselves to be professional writers and artists, working at home, or by enrolling in some educational institution as correspondence students. But even then members of professions and students must belong to the respective trade union or show educational progress to be maintained on the school rolls.

A few young unmarried women may obtain employment

as private secretaries of their influential lovers. But none of this is professional prostitution, in the Western sense.

Outwardly, today, Soviet society is decorous and even puritancial; sex is kept away from all public places, but sexual promiscuity in private may be just as prevalent as in Western societies. It is possible that some of those activities are protest against the restrictions imposed by socialist societies upon their citizens. But it is incorrect to assume that all such sex activities have political connotations directed against the socialist economic and political order. All over the world there are protests against any order at all. It is a purely psychological phenomenon, probably rooted in biology, with young generations growing impatient to elbow the older ones out of the way. Sexual promiscuity might be one form of protest against the system, but it is probably less dangerous than, for instance, physical violence. Above all it provides an emotional release for explosive pent-up anxieties. Therefore it might be beneficial rather than harmful for the stability of any society.

Extra-marital sex for women is becoming more and more accepted by more people in the Soviet Union as a normal, salutary development. This need not worry Soviet planners. No complete liberation of woman is possible without liberating her from sexual restrictions and taboos. It is also biologically normal that it is woman who should call the sex "shots" since physiologically sex has a different and more profound meaning for her than for man. And with her emotional wild oats safely sown before marriage, she might enter it as a better partner for man, and potentially better future mother to her children, than if she were rushed into it by pent-up sex urges or by economic reasons.

This question is not currently popular with Soviet legislators, sociologists, and demographers who consider stable families to be the mainstay of the society. But is extramarital and premarital sex experience detrimental to marriage as an institution? Or is premarital sex a beneficial factor, preparing young people for sexual responsibilities?

Whatever the answer, the Soviet girl need no longer be forced into marriage as the only traditional or legal outlet for her sexual urges. It is her unalienable right to order her sex life in any manner she wishes, in or out of marriage.

Drying geological samples in the Siberian taiga. All geological teams are mixed—boys and girls work and live under conditions of close intimacy which would be embarrassing elsewhere. Many marriages result, romances flourish, but any male aggressiveness would result in expulsion from the team —or worse. The law protects women, but in any event Russian girls seem to know very well how to protect themselves.

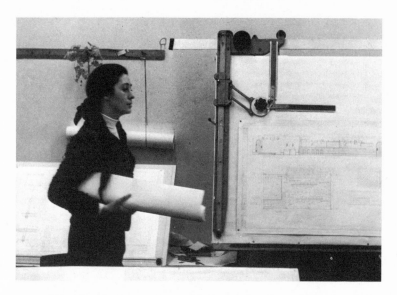

Kira Soshinskaya, the architect of the Central Institute of Business Building Construction. (1968)

Alexandra Karaseva, the captain of a fishing boat operating in the waters of Kamchatka, in the Siberian Northeast. Many women are engaged in commercial fishing—an occupation once reserved to men. There are fishing boat crews composed entirely of young girls.

10.   Red is Beautiful

In the old Slavic language a single word means both red and beautiful; and in modern Russian the word *prekrasny* (very red) means beautiful. And in Russian folk fairy tales *krasnaya-devitza* (red girl) means beautiful girl. The fabulous Red Square in Moscow was so named long before the Revolution. It simply means a beautiful square.

As we all know, beauty is in the eye of the beholder; and standards of feminine beauty vary widely. In some places in Africa women with monstrous saucer lips would evoke wolf whistles sooner than Raquel Welch or Brigitte Bardot. Sickeningly deformed women's feet were once considered extremely beautiful in China, and until recently girls with their breasts so tightly bound that they were undiscernable were in vogue in Japan.

In the Middle Ages women with protruding soft stomachs were very much admired—Rubens immortalized this trend. And even Venus of Milo, coming to life today, would be hardly called beautiful by accepted Western standards.

Almost all foreign travelers coming to Russia today comment on the general lack of attractiveness of Russian women, particularly when they are past their first youth. Most are much too heavy by Western standards, with massive busts and posteriors. But there is a deeply rooted feeling among Russian men that Russian women are the most beautiful in the world.

There are women beautiful to Western eyes in the Soviet Union, very many of them. In some areas of the country, both men and women are extremely handsome: the French

Larousse Encyclopedia considers the Georgians the most handsome race in the world. Indeed the Georgians, particularly the men—the legendary Georgian princes—were collecting American heiresses by the score when they appeared in America and Europe after the Revolution. Young women from the Moslem regions of Central Asia are also very handsome, some even extremely beautiful. There are Ukrainian girls who could hold their own in any beauty contest, particularly if they are fully clothed—their thighs might appear a bit too sturdy for a Miss Universe judge.

But to a Russian man, these cannot hold a candle to the traditional Russian beauty with massive legs, breasts, and posterior, and with a slightly snub nose and flaming red cheeks on her round face.

Traditionally, physical strength has been equated with desirability where women are concerned. It is not for nothing that in common Russian parlance the word *zdorovaya* ("healthy") is synonymous with strong. This explains why Russian women, until very recently, did not worry about layers of fat accumulating all over their bodies—they were the symbol of health, vigor, and promising work potential.

This goes back to the peasant society where woman was more valued for her ability to work alongside her man than for her looks. "One does not drink water out of woman's face," according to the old Russian proverb. So on the peasant matrimonial market monumental legs and broad muscular back were more valued than a graceful figure. If such a girl had a pretty face as well, with flaming round cheeks and sparkling eyes, she would be a paragon of desirability—and would have no dearth of peasant lads pining for her. But a sturdy body with generous curves were the first requisite; and facial beauty, though eagerly admired, was a secondary consideration.

The bitter climate and a diet composed almost entirely

of starches and fats did the rest. Fat was a protection from cold, supplied by nature; and starchy food: bread, millet, and potatoes, were often the only food available to peasant families for months and months at a stretch. Many generations of this have produced a typical Slav peasant woman, strong and resilient, capable of coping with practically any discomfort and hardship and with the hardest possible work—often pulling a plow along with a horse, *if* a horse was available. Such women were deeply respected and admired in old Russian villages, and evoked sexual appreciation.

The Slav peasant woman had to be a good dependable breeder. It was universally believed that only large sturdy women were capable of producing children standing any chance of survival amidst the catastrophic infant mortality rate which was common to all peasant areas. And children were all important in peasant economy. They were the investment against the frightening future when their parents would exhaust their physical capacities of survival, and would become their children's dependents. And they were valuable helpmates long before then—usually they were put to work while still very young. It was not unusual to see a boy of five tending geese, and a girl the same age feeding chickens and helping her mother with household chores.

Genetically, the present Russian society is a peasant one. The once-privileged classes were almost totally destroyed or driven into exile during the Revolution and the civil war. These privileged classes had had little in common genetically with the vast masses of peasants. For centuries they lived and bred separately, and had developed a totally different set of standards and code of behavior. They often produced truly beautiful women who graced ballrooms, theatres, and society salons; but who would get no second glance from an average peasant man. It is no exaggeration to say that they had no more social intercourse with peasants than South African

Boer landlords have with their Bantu farmhands, even though they spoke more or less the same language and shared the same religion and history.

There is no such thing as a Russian ethnic type, or even a Slav type. There are dozens and dozens of types, even among closely related ethnic groups. Northern Russians are often blond and blue eyed, and have rough facial features, while Ukrainians are mostly dark-eyed and have finer faces. But these are only generalizations. The Slavs are notorious cross-breeders, having no idea of any racial superiority; many of them have mixed blood. Mongol domination for almost three hundred years left its indelible marks. "Scratch a Russian and you will find a Tartar," Napoleon said; and he was not far from truth.

Many Russian women, particularly young ones, are beautiful, but the main feature of their attractiveness often lies in their *oboyannye*—the untranslatable Russian word describing charm, personality, and enchantment rolled into one. Millions of televiewers throughout the world were treated to the display of this elusive quality in Munich when a young Russian gymnast, Olga Korbut, became an undisputed darling of the Olympics after a few minutes' performance. But then Olga is a modern Soviet girl, and a gymnast; she is not typical of the traditionally husky Russian girls.

If one must generalize, he can say that the majority of Russian women today are not very beautiful by Western standards; almost all foreign visitors to Russia would agree. And until very recently the women cared little about altering this situation and particularly about watching their figures. They had no particular encouragement to do so from their men.

Peasant standards of attractiveness continued through the Revolution, the hard reconstruction, the war and postwar years, roughly until the 1960's; a long period when women were a primary source of hard labor, and when their physical durability was an all-important factor for the country's economy. Many things which West European and American women would consider absolutely essential such as stockings, brassieres, underwear, and even the most primitive toiletries, were simply not available. A single cotton dress and a pair of canvas *tapochkas,* or heelless slippers, had to do in summer; and a pair of felt boots, a heavy shawl and an overcoat, often remade from a soldier's greatcoat, were added during bitter winters. During these winters when women worked outside, felling trees, digging ditches, or laying bricks, a good layer of body fat and a plate of hot thick soup with pieces of floating pork fat would go a long way towards making their lives bearable.

All this has been changing during the last decade, and oddly enough, in some indirect way, this change can be charged to women's liberation and emancipation. These changes have proceeded in a diametrically opposite direction from the present trend of eliminating the degrading symbols of femininity much in vogue among women's lib militants in Western Europe and America. In the Soviet Union it has taken the form of a return to feminity and this movement has been spearheaded by the young, intelligent and well-educated women.

This trend of feminization of the Soviet woman has had official government sanction since an increased birthrate and a strong Soviet family have become important to Soviet demographers and legislators. Some of the most recent labor laws, for instance those limiting the employment of women, would have been met with howls of protest by militant feminists in Europe and America. They are criticized by some women in the Soviet Union, but are generally accepted as a progressive development reflecting the general rise of prosperity. They are supported by women's organizations and trade unions.

To achieve an increased birthrate, sex had to be diverted

back into productive channels. It had to be personalized once
again, rather than allowed to remain casual, a woman had to
become *the* woman, the one and only, mysteriously alluring,
unique and keenly desirable. She had to become attractive to
man's libido rather than to his class consciousness, to become
a treasured item which would evoke male biological possessiveness.

Throughout the ages this has been achieved by a sort of
physiological fraud—woman has used every possible guile to
present herself as some special and highly desirable piece of
sex merchandise with the aid of clothes and cosmetics and
personal grooming to set off her best features and camou-
flaging the less attractive ones. The same trend can be seen in
Russia today, though its avowed aims are different.

Anyone visiting large Soviet cities today will note a large
number of well groomed, well made up, and attractively
dressed young women, their hair clean and their hands mani-
cured. Older women are still often heavy, drab, and even
sloppy; but it is quite unusual to see a fat girl or young woman.
Fat has lost its allure for young men at least. And this trend
is spreading throughout the country.

Three years ago I had an opportunity to travel in Siberia,
and was impressed by the appearance of young women even
in the most remote corners of that enormous and still very
rough land. Among other places, I visited a rest home for
hydroelectric dam workers set deep in the virgin *taiga*. There
were perhaps fifty or sixty young women there, and every
morning they would line up in front of the scales in the lobby
weighing themselves. My companion and I made a special
check, and not one of them was overweight by the most exact-
ing Western standards. One tipped the scales at 170 pounds,
but she was over six feet tall. Women in their forties and
older were heavy, two or three exceedingly so, but not the
girls. And all of them had their hair attractively styled, their

clothes were neat, and all used cosmetics including perfume. My Soviet companion was particularly impressed—he swore to me that when he had visited the same place only five years before, things were vastly different. "They must have gone mad," he commented. Being a fairly young man he was very surprised, and by no means unpleasantly so. "I am almost sorry I am married."

As everything in a socialist society, this has been carefully planned. There are probably more beauty salons in Moscow today than in most European or American cities; and the government-controlled prices are fully within reach of women with even the lowest incomes. All beauty aids are plentiful but their quality is probably below average Western standards. But then their prices are often ridiculously low. The cosmetic industries are state subsidized with the result that it is often cheaper to buy a bottle of fairly good Soviet perfume in Moscow than a pair of man's cotton socks. Nylon stockings are plentiful, but still rather expensive; and some items of ladies' underwear displayed in shops are coquettishly frilly, often made of natural Turkestan silk which, incidentally, is held in lesser regard by Soviet shoppers than synthetic fabrics. But that is one of the quirks of Soviet merchandising: everything scarce, new, and made abroad is considered chic and is in strong demand. I was told in Siberia that an English woman traveling in a nylon fake-fur coat exchanged it in Bratsk for a mink one; and the proud possessor of that imitation foreign luxury then became an undisputed fashion queen of her community.

This might be an exaggeration; but during one of our trips, my wife brought with her a large, plastic shopping bag of flaming red color. She was so annoyed by women stopping her in Moscow streets and begging her to sell it that she finally gave it to a hotel chambermaid, whereupon the stout middle-aged peasant woman disintegrated into hysterics of gratitude.

Such items as miniskirts (locally known as *micro-youbka's*) and very tight sweaters have become very popular with young girls; and Soviet-made bikinis are designed to cover very little. Displaying a woman's body to advantage has ceased to be a sign of bourgeois decadence. Within limits, of course. There are still no strip-tease shows and no topless waitresses.

Comparing Soviet women to women one meets on Fifth Avenue, Knightsbridge or the Champs Elysees is quite unfair. One should compare them with women in a worker's quarter of any large city, for Soviet women are in a vast majority just such working women. In monetary terms even professional women in the Soviet Union, such as doctors, engineers, and architects, earn less than American cleaning women or London chars. This is partly offset by certain social advantages, but the disparity is still there. Within this framework, modern Soviet woman has done herself proud in recent years in her striking progress back to attractive femininity.

This is not accidental, but a part of a concentrated propaganda and economic drive to improve the image of the Soviet women. Fashion designers are pampered in today's Russia; and one of them, Viacheslav Zaitzev, has earned for himself an international reputation. However—men are still dressed rather shabbily; and men's clothes are expensive and often poorly made, compared to women's. But then women have always been a mainstay of the Soviet Union, both economically and morally—and they richly deserve their present leading position in the Red sex market.

Did we say sex market? This is perhaps an inaccurate expression for a society where all private trade is illegal. But Soviet woman does not sell herself, the state does this for her, in a number of ways. The latest labor legislation is certainly curtailing her earning potential. Other ways are more subtle, such as the recognition of true, romantic love in literature and other art forms; the stress of gallantry, chivalry, and male good manners as social virtues; and the appearance of scantly-clad beautiful girls with blinding smiles on travel posters and, yes, even on calendars. Add the suppression of anything which might give the Soviet woman a wrong image. When I was selecting photographs of women in Moscow I was politely, but insistently requested not to use any which showed unattractive women. "Since our women are so beautiful why show old, fat monsters? Show Soviet women as they *really* are. After all, socialism produces happiness, and happiness is the best beauty aid."

One need only visit any Intourist office and get their publicity brochures. Every one of them shows a smiling young woman, always beautiful; and those advertising summer resorts show these girls in various stages of undress—sometimes quite daring stages.

Traveling in Siberia with a photographer three years ago, I was also asked not to photograph any old and unattractive women. "There are too many beautiful girls in Siberia to waste film on ugly ones."

In other words, Red is beautiful.

I promised to comply with such requests to the limits of my conscience as a favorably objective journalist, a peculiar Soviet definition composed of two contradictory terms. But I must say with all honesty that I saw more beautiful girls in Siberia than anywhere else in the Soviet Union. Perhaps this impression is created by the fact that women in Siberia are predominately young. And young women throughout the Soviet Union have certainly made a gigantic leap back to femininity in the fifteen years since I first visited the country.

Many of these girls, properly decked out, are quite pretty, and some even very beautiful by any standards. Some explain this by a greatly improved diet, and this may be partly true. But the absence of all cosmetics and fine clothing probably

exaggerated the impression of the Soviet girl being an un-
appetizing dish. Beauty is difficult to detect under torn over-
alls and in weather-beaten faces, calloused hands with broken
nails, and in sturdy bare legs with bulging muscles. It is surprising what a pair of sheer nylons can do for women's legs,
and a pretty dress for their bodies.

But the deadliest enemy to Slavic women is fat—the
natural predisposition for accumulating it all over their bodies
starting at thirty-five or even thirty. By the time they reach
forty they are usually fat as pigs, and make not the slightest
effort to reduce.

It has been said that after many years of food shortages
and some real starvation years, the people in the Soviet Union
turned into food addicts in the 1960's. Slavs have always been
ferocious eaters whenever they could get hold of food. *Calorie*
has never been a popular word in Russia—and still isn't. Unfortunately the most abundant foods are starches, particularly bread of which all Russians are extremely fond. Next
comes thick soups with layers of fat on the top, always the
mainstay of the Russian diet.

The shock of having an abundance of food has worn off
by now, but Russian appetites have not noticeably decreased.
Having dinner at a Russian home is a gastronomic catastrophe, if one cares at all about food intake. Not only is food
abundant; but the pressure to gorge oneself is terrific. One
just cannot beg off without offending the hostess.

One can only hope that young Soviet girls who have discovered their figures will be able to hold that line, and will
not slide back into the traditional food intemperance which
was largely responsible for the flesh explosion among their
mothers—quite aside from any genetic predisposition to obesity. The attitude of young men could do more than calorie
charts; and their attitude seems to be changing, though some
young men would still prefer girls fleshily endowed.

The girls still seem to be unconscious of the dangers of obesity. Once in the Ukraina hotel in Moscow I watched for a rather long time an extremely beautiful young girl operating the elevator. She was pleasantly plump, but not fat; and she had a pair of truly beautiful legs—rather a rarity among Slav women. Every third or fourth trip she would open and lock the elevator door, despite loud protests of people waiting to be taken up, and dash to the buffet counter in the lobby to buy a sausage or smoked sturgeon sandwich which she would take to her car to nibble on during her up-and-down trips. When one of the waiting men objected and complained to a fat motherly woman who sat in the lobby, presumably regulating the elevator traffic, the woman just shrugged and said: "Leave her alone. She is very unhappy today. She had a fight with her husband."

So apparently she was trying to drown her unhappiness in smoked fish. One can only hope the quarrel was eventually patched up, and the beautiful girl has saved her figure.

Watching young women eat breakfast in Moscow hotels can be an unnerving experience. Breakfast has always been one of the principal meals in the Russian gastronomic scheme of things, but both Russian men and women overdo it. I actually saw one woman consume six fried eggs, two large helpings of frankfurters with sauerkraut and potato salad, eight slices of buttered white bread, three sweet rolls, and top it all with a three-ounce glass of Armenian cognac—the favorite morning drink in Russia. She was already well on the way of becoming a full-blown Russian beauty. Her face was truly beautiful—but not her legs!

Would the present drive back to femininity lure young Soviet men into marriages and child-producing? Men had been spoiled by many years of the male shortage and had developed a rather casual attitude to women who, until recently, were in over-abundant supply. This casual attitude persists, and it has been worrying Soviet demographers. It is still normal to see girls dancing together during social functions while men would just stand around and look, or . . . dance with one another. This is a throwback to old peasant ways when any physical contact between the sexes in public was not considered proper: all old Russian folk dances exclude such contact.

Strange as it may seem, another reason for the casual and even slightly contemptuous attitude of young men towards girls was the intimate proximity into which the sexes were drawn during the reconstruction period and also during the war. In large industrial projects in the Far North and in Siberia young men and women were thrown together with utter disregard to sex, and it was not unusual for young girls to be temporarily lodged in men's barracks, and vice versa, until the proper segregation could be effected. And during the war girls and young women fought alongside male soldiers, eating and sleeping with them, and by all accounts such proximity did not lead to any sexual excesses—on the contrary, it caused the loss of that mutual sex curiosity which is one element of sex attraction.

This is changing now. With the rising prosperity, and particularly with the easing of the housing situation, the sexes once again are becoming segregated. Gone is the time when two or three couples would occupy the same room. But some indiscrimination in this sphere still persists: even for long railway trips, sleeping compartments are allocated without regard to the passengers' sexes, and in smaller towns a single toilet in hotels and restaurants is used by men and women.

But in recent years, woman has become more and more distant and mysterious as far as young men are concerned. This goes a long way towards creation of sex attraction. Modern Soviet girls, with the age-old female instinct, are becoming coquettish and a little coy, demanding courting: Male gallantry and chivalry are currently very much in demand among them. They demand respect and are getting it; they more and more refuse to be taken for granted.

Absence of out-and-out pornography is also going for them in this respect. Nothing deadens male sex interest more than the repeated exposure to completely naked female bodies —sex thrives on fantasies. The current vogue in American, English, and Scandinavian sex magazines of leaving nothing at all to the imagination in their girlie displays has not been permitted to penetrate the Soviet Union, and this has greatly helped Soviet woman on her way back to feminine allure. While legs can be fully exposed currently in Soviet art and photography, breasts, and particularly nipples, are still taboo except in those situations when a woman is shown breast-feeding her child—which Russian women often do in public, particularly in rural areas.

Pubic hair is never shown or mentioned, not even in underground pornography which has made its appearance in large cities. (Among Moslem women of Central Asia and the Caucasus traditionally pubic hair had been removed before a woman was married, often by a barbaric method of smearing it with clay, letting it harden, and then pulling the hair out with its roots along with the dry clay. This custom, I am told, is no longer followed, just as circumcision which had been a religious must among Moslem men is rarely performed nowadays. The operation now may be performed only by certified surgeons. This is why many Jewish boys in the Soviet Union, even in strictly Orthodox families, are uncircumcised; the rabbis, unless they are surgically trained, are no longer permitted to do this.)

Full female nudity is sometimes permitted in sculpture, and it has appeared recently for fleeting moments in films— usually outside of the purely sexual context. In the Kon- chalovsky film entitled *The First Teacher* the heroine appears completely unclothed with her pubic hair removed, historically correct since she was a Moslem girl. In the beautiful *Andrei Rublev,* a whole flock of naked females graces the screen for a few seconds. Both scenes have survived Soviet film censors who can be merciless when it comes to even faintly sexy scenes. Even kissing must be comradely rather than passionate, and without any suggestion of depth. Love, pure romantic love.

(But the Russian attitude towards nudity has always been ambiguous. I distinctly remember, as a small child, being taken by more mature friends in a rowboat to some secluded river beach near St. Petersburg where nude mixed bathing was going on. Whole families were frolicking on the sand without a stitch on. Even then, being probably six years old, I was disturbed and appalled by the sight of mature women with masses of flesh hanging all over them wading ankle-deep in the water. This would not have been permitted in the Soviet Union today; and so, in some areas at least, the Tsar's Russia was more revolutionary than the present Soviet society.)

How does this back to femininity trend among Soviet women today square up with their liberation and emancipation? Isn't that a definite step back in woman's progress towards a complete equality with men in every sphere of life?

I had a long discussion about this with a Russian woman of keen intelligence—the same lady who asked me not to use her name because it was unimportant. She was probably a member of the Communist Party, but she was free from the pragmatic dogmatism which so often comes with the Party membership. She spoke and read English; and she was familiar with the work of Betty Friedan, Gloria Steinem, Kate Millett, Germaine Greer and other women's lib militants; and she was not afraid to criticize some aspects of her government's handling of human problems, particularly those concerning women.

But as it often happens in the Soviet Union, it is one thing to listen to complaints of Soviet citizens about imperfections of their system, and quite another to criticize any aspects of this system in their presence. They often become offended if one simply repeats the complaints which they themselves had voiced only a minute before. My interlocutor was not that stupid; but she was instantly on her guard when I started questioning her about some seeming contradictions in the current Soviet trend towards feminization of Soviet woman.

Obviously I cannot quote her verbatim since I took no notes during this conversation (don't ever pull out a notebook while speaking to any Soviet citizen—that is the surest way to make them freeze on you!), but the gist of her arguments was as follows: "Aw for God's sake!" she said. (God is often called upon in modern Soviet parlance.) "Can you tell me in what way being feminine and attractive interferes with woman's freedom or equality? Let me tell you something: in our society this is a direct result of woman's liberation. Soviet woman no longer has to be rough and masculine to prove her equality with men—she has already proved it; and now she can afford to be feminine. As a woman and a doctor I can state categorically that every normal young woman, with balanced sexuality, and not emotionally disturbed, wants to be admired—and yes, even desired by men around her. And so displaying her best physical qualities is an absolutely normal biological urge in no way interfering with her equal rights with men in any and all spheres of life.

"It is different in your world. There woman does this in order to sell herself, to get a good husband or a rich lover. There it is a matter of economics with her. But not with our woman. Of course she wants to attract the best man she can—good-looking, clean, strong, and intelligent, and because there are few of such ideal men, there is a competition. But this is a biological competition, not an economic one. She knows that men are sooner attracted to good-looking, neat, well-dressed and well-groomed women than to sloppy ones reeking of onions and sweat; and she does her best to attract the best man. But what is important is that neither one of them can buy the other; and so a woman by displaying her best physiological advantages does not prostitute herself."

"Prostitution is an ambiguous term," I said. "Do you want to tell me that if a girl has a choice between two equally desirable men, and one of them is a factory worker and another a factory director, this would not influence her choice?"

"Probably, but how many factory directors are there? And then her choice would be prostitution only if she loved the worker, but married the director only for his position. And there are still whores among our women, but we are discussing an average Soviet girl—not special cases. In a vast majority of cases, the Soviet girl knows that by marrying she will not materially improve her economic position—on the contrary, by having children she is bound to worsen it. We did succeed in eliminating—almost eliminating—economics from sex, including marriage. And this is a gigantic step towards woman's real liberation. Nothing enslaves woman so much as financial dependence on man—in or out of marriage. Some time ago you had debutante balls where well-scrubbed, beautifully dressed, and sweet-smelling young girls were put on display for prospective buyers—just like slave girls were once displayed in Oriental markets. Thank God, such barbarism does not, and cannot exist with us. It went out with dowries and conjugal rights—our young girls would not even believe that such savageries once existed in Russia when sex was often the sole means for a woman to earn her food and her lodging.

"Of course we want our women to be feminine and attractive. We want them to marry and bear children. We want them to be decent. We don't consider that behaving like a whore proves woman's equality. When your women militants use such words as 'fuck,' 'cock,' and 'cunt' [She used the Russian equivalents, of course] they only prove their deep-seated inferiority, and nothing else. Oh, perhaps this is necessary in your society in order to attract attention, to create publicity, as you call it, but we are past this stage. Our women do not have to swear like men to prove that they are as good as men; they have already proved this, and no one today even questions it. They can afford to look and act as women—and no one takes it as a sign of their inferiority. And it *is* pleasant to be good-looking, to dress well, to have clean hands and hair, and to smell nicely. With us this is a manner of good social manners, and nothing else."

"But what about those restrictive laws which exclude women from many trades and professions?" I asked.

"First of all, women are excluded from very few—only those which hurt their health. Oh, I know that your militant feminists claim that there are no such thing as man's and woman's work, that every woman can do anything a man could do, except producing sperm. And when they speak about woman's *right* to do man's work, they are trying to establish a principle. They still have to win this right. But our women have established this principle and this right long ago. They worked in mines, dug ditches and canals, and loaded and unloaded trains and ships. But to claim that an average woman can do such work just as well as an average man is a physiological absurdity—one look at an anatomical chart would prove it. No, an average woman cannot compete with an average man in certain things just as she cannot start producing spermatozoa. And why should she? That does not prove her inferiority to man. Nature has endowed her with other capabilities, infinitely more valuable and important than digging coal.

"You see, in your society you are still talking about the battle of the sexes. But we have eliminated the economic

reasons for such fratricidal struggle, and have proved that
cooperation of the sexes pays much higher dividends to society. When it was necessary, our women did the hardest work,
often damaging their health in the process, so there is no question of principle any longer. They would again do this in
emergency. But there is no emergency now, so they need not
ruin their health and their capacity of functioning as women
to prove that they are liberated. Our women are not only
women, but fully responsible members of our society. And it
is the duty of the society to protect their members' health, and
to manage its human resources in the best and most productive
ways for everyone's benefit. It has been medically proved that
certain work damages woman's health, and hampers her ability to function biologically as a normal woman. And her functioning as a woman is infinitely more valuable to society than
her digging coal—that is a flagrant misuse of her abilities and
her talents."

"But doesn't this lower the average earning capacity of
women in comparison with men?" I knew that this was a sore
point—many women have complained to me about this. And
so my friend hesitated a little before answering.

"Yes, it does—in monetary terms. Of course, a miner
earns four times more than, for instance, a bacteriologist, and
more than a doctor. But competition in monetary terms is not
nearly as important with us as it is with you. We don't com-
pute a person's worth by the amount of money he has. With
lifelong guaranteed work and basic security for everyone,
money has become less important with us than with you. And
there is another way of looking at it. A miner's work is unpleasant and very dull, and extremely hard, taking everything
out of him, and leaving him with little spare energy to improve himself and his qualifications by additional education.
So it is only normal and just that he is paid more than, let us
say, a girl laboratory researcher who has every opportunity

in the world to study and to improve her qualifications in order to become a doctor or a full-fledged scientist. I really can't imagine such a girl abandoning her work and going into a mine just for the sake of a few more rubles, and by so doing ruining her health and her future. And if she is stupid enough to try it, it is society's duty to stop her. Don't forget: she has already proved her right and her ability to dig coal—where there were no men to do it—so there is no principle involved. I think we are doing a great honor to our women by, along with insuring their economic independence, diverting their abilities and their talents into more valuable and productive channels."

"Do all women feel like you do?"

"No, of course not. Many of them complain, and sometimes, rightly so. Many laws concerning women are still imperfect—mostly because most of them are made by men. But what all foreigners seem to forget that we are a society in transition, and that our present system is strictly an interim one. We are moving and building towards communism, remember? There are many imperfections in our present setup, and we are constantly developing new growing pains. But those pains only prove that we are growing, that we are not sclerotic, and they are constantly corrected to the limit of our economic abilities. Some women yell that their rights are being restricted, but every organized society has some restrictive laws. Don't you have some laws restricting employment of women?"

"Well, in America, for instance, there is a law forbidding discrimination against women," I said. "It is called the Civil Rights Act, and under it no woman can be denied any employment because of her sex, for so long as she has proper qualifications for any job."

I didn't know this," my friend admitted. "And how many women coal miners or locomotive drivers have you?"

"Probably none, but the principle is there."

"Principle again! We are beyond that stage here. Perhaps we were fortunate. Our women were forced to get out of their secure conjugal beds, as they then called them, and produce the bread with their own hands before they could eat it, or give it to their children. In the beginning this must have been a shock to them—like being thrown into the water without knowing how to swim. They floundered, and many of them went under, but most of them have learned how to swim, and have been swimming very well ever since. That was before my time; but I know that for the girls of my generation the very idea that our future husbands might support us was utterly ridiculous, almost obscene. And until your women realize that sitting home, breeding children, and being supported by their husbands is the most degrading form of prostitution, all anti-discrimination laws would be meaningless. This might sound paradoxical, but women's liberation starts with the liberation of men from legal and traditional obligations of supporting their wives. Without economic independence—earned independence—there can be no equality: there are no rights without responsibilities. For as long as women keep selling sex, they will be slaves, and will be treated as slaves, and deservedly so."

"Perhaps," I said. "I know that Soviet woman has made a remarkable progress during the last fifty years. And this is why your new Code of Marriage and Family struck me as being very conservative, almost patriarchal. There is nothing revolutionary about it, and it would have never satisfied our feminists."

"I suppose it wouldn't, because your feminists are still dealing with ideals, and not realities. And they think that revolution means only destruction. But then comes the time when everything has been destroyed, the ground has been cleared, and the new building must be built. This building process can also be revolutionary for as long as you're building something radically new, but here one must work with realities, and not mere ideals."

"Surrendering some of the ideals?"

"No, but combining them with realities. Lenin said that one must be a realistic idealist, and an idealistic realist, is one wanted the revolution to succeed and last. We had our destructive, anarchistic period; but it had to be stopped when there was nothing left to destroy. And some old practical methods had to be resorted to again."

"Such as luring woman back into legal marriage and childbirth?"

My friend was becoming annoyed. "That's a dishonest argument. First of all no one is luring anyone anywhere. Any woman has a perfect right to remain single and have twenty abortions if she wants them. What we were trying to do was to create the conditions under which a normal woman can enjoy having a family and children. I say enjoy because those things are a biological necessity for almost all normal women. We are trying to strengthen the family; but the question is, what family? The family in which husband and wife are completely economically independent from each other, sharing the same rights and responsibilities. The code does provide that man must support his wife if she is sick or disabled, but it also provides that woman must support her husband under similar circumstances. And that both have absolutely equal responsibilities towards their children. If they divorce and children remain with their father, the mother must pay him alimony for their support. Is that patriarchal? We are not trying to bring back the old marriage where woman sleeps with a man in exchange for her food and the roof over her head."

"I've been told that some Russian women stay at home."

"Yes, but usually only temporarily when their children need their attention. There are very few women who would

stop working permanently when they are married. I don't
know, ten percent perhaps, but in time even that percentage
will disappear. Children often interfere with women's professional lives now; but that will be changed in time. We can't
do everything at once. So far we have freed woman from
economic dependence on man; that is an accomplished fact.
No woman *has* to sleep with a man because he supports her,
and if some still do, that's their free choice. In time woman
will be also freed from household drudgery and the necessity
to devote her time to children: the state will assume the full
responsibility for them. This is still our tomorrow, but at least
we know that this tomorrow *will* come. Women themselves
will make it come. For make no mistake: our women are a
dynamic creative force in this country. They are not in it for
a free ride. They have built it along with their men—with
their hands and their brains. They have discovered the joy of
economic independence, coupled with lifelong security, which
they have earned with their own labor, and nothing in the
world can force them back into their former position of sex
pariahs."

"Your women are remarkable," I conceded, "But aren't
you afraid that with rising prosperity and the return to traditional femininity, they might lose some of their moral stamina
and become corrupted by their new easy lives?"

"Easy lives!" my friend smiled. "Life is never easy for
anyone taking an active part in it, like our girls are, only to
parasites. And we have eliminated parasitism as a legal life
form. And as to femininity, as you call it, that is any woman's
biological right. Our women have won their economic independence, and proved their equality, so they can afford to take
a bit of time off to dress and look well, and take a better care
of their bodies. And if our girls wear miniskirts and tight
sweaters, use lipstick and nail polish, and flirt with men—
more power to them. Believe me they are not doing this to

win or catch husbands, as you call it, but to attract the best possible partners in life—partners, mind you, and not lords and masters. And that is every woman's birthright."

"One last question," I said. "What would you advise our women's lib militants to do in order to win the rights which they claim have been denied them?"

My friend thought for a moment. "To stop fighting biology, and start fighting the economic system which uses biology to enslave them. To stop fighting men who are just as badly trapped by the oppressive economy as they are. That's a wasteful fight because it divides the oppressed instead of uniting them against the oppressor. And above all, to stop regarding their sex as a salable commodity, and start enjoying it as free human beings. And, of course, to fight the conditions which make this shameful commerce possible."

"In other words, start a revolution?"

"No, continue the one which is going on. Your world is changing just as fast as ours, only in a different way. Perhaps revolution in our sense is impossible with you, and even un-necessary—you will get there in your own way, replacing the present setup with something infinitely better. And tell them to stay as clean, neat, feminine, and beautiful as they can—there is too much ugliness in the world as it is."

It is easy to be a feminist in Russia. The vast majority of Soviet men are feminists, deeply respecting their women's performance since the revolution which rescued them from the medieval oppression, and forced them into a brand new world. And it is my honest opinion, as a favorably objective observer, that they have proved themselves fully worthy of this rare historical opportunity.

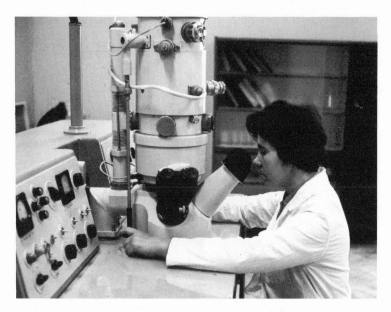

Galina Shevchenko, a young scientist of Siberia, head of the chemico-physical lab at Achinsk.

These girls are highly qualified experts at the Khabarovsk chemico-pharmaceutical plant. They are choosing young deer antlers "in velvet" suitable for the preparation of a highly-regarded medicinal tonic preparation called pantakrin. Both are medical school graduates continuing their studies at night.

11. Conclusion

This work does not pretend to be an exhaustive study of a large and complicated theme. It was drawn from available official statistics and documents: no extensive grass-roots survey was conducted. However scores of Soviet women—and men—were talked to during extensive travels throughout the huge country.

The task has been complicated by the enormous ethnic diversity of the Soviet Union. But since the Russian language and culture have penetrated all ethnic groups composing the Soviet nation, and since the laws regulating human relations are basically identical throughout the country (with only a few local deviations) the study of the position of woman within the Soviet Russian Federation, the Ukraine, and Belorussia, the three Slavic republics, reflects to some extent the position of woman throughout the country. Generalizations are dangerous, but in a work of this size they are unavoidable.

What have been the achievements of Soviet woman during the last fifty years?

Before answering this sweeping question one must consider the starting point of this process.

In the tsar's Russia women throughout the country shared the common lack of legal and civic rights. Also, among the peasant masses, which comprised over 80 percent of the entire population, almost total lack of education. Very few Russian peasant women could read and write, and in the Moslem regions of the country and among smaller ethnic groups, illiteracy among women was universal.

The Revolution disfranchised and largely destroyed all the privileged and better-educated classes, considerably lower-

ing the overall literacy figure among women. At the end of
the first year of the Revolution, at least 90 percent of all
women in the country were illiterate.

Many of these women were also deeply steeped in old
religious traditions which proclaimed the divine superiority
of man. The vast majority of them had no trades or professions, and their only work experience came from working in
the fields.

To compare the position of Russian peasant woman at
the turn of the century with that of a woman in America and
in Western European countries of that time is incorrect. A
more accurate picture would be obtained by the comparison
between a Russian peasant woman before the Revolution, and
a peasant woman in feudal Europe of the Middle Ages. Only
then would the achievements of Soviet women become truly
meaningful.

For the sake of comprehensive summation, we may break
the original question into several separate queries each covering a specific area of human activity, and try to arrive at objective answers indicating Soviet woman's position today in
these areas.

1. Legal equality.

One of the very first decrees promulgated by the Soviet
government, and reputedly personally drafted by Lenin, proclaimed complete and absolute equality of the sexes in all
legal matters, without a single exception. All old discrimina-
tory laws, usually based on church canons, were annulled;
and religious denominations were stripped of all legal authority.

It had taken considerable time to eradicate ancient customs and traditions, particularly in rural areas; but as of today
Soviet woman has achieved a complete equality with man not
only in law, but in fact.

2. Education and culture.

Soviet woman, starting from zero at the time of the Revolution, has made the most remarkable progress in this area. Today there is no woman in the Soviet Union below the age of fifty who is illiterate; and the average level of education of Soviet women compares favorably with the most advanced Western societies. The percentage of women doctors, engineers, architects, jurists, and workers in all areas of science in the Soviet Union today greatly exceeds such percentages in all Western societies.

Until recently the number of women students in all Soviet universities exceeded that of men; but during the last few years it has fallen slightly below the male-student level. The latest estimate of the disparity between the sexes in universities is 53 to 47 percent in favor of men. With no demographic disparity between the sexes in the younger generations, many young Soviet women marry fairly early, and some abandon their studies after the birth of the first child. However almost all such women continue some sort of education through correspondence courses offered by all colleges and universities. So the number of women students attending classes does not represent the total number of women receiving education.

In all cultural activities women predominate in the Soviet Union. Among teachers in all grades, lecturers, art students, theatre and museum workers, librarians, artists, etc. women are a majority; and in some fields such as education, in an overwhelming majority.

3. Employment.

The Soviet constitution declares work not merely the right, but the obligation of every able-bodied citizen regardless of sex, and guarantees such employment, according to the person's qualifications, throughout his or her active work life.

All Soviet women work at some periods of their lives—there are few exceptions. The number of permanently non-working women is very small; usually they are mothers of numerous children. Bringing up children is, by law, a socially beneficial occupation.

Women enjoy many legal privileges in the employment area, such as fully paid pre- and postnatal leaves, leaves for taking care of their sick children, and optional unpaid leaves without losing job seniority for a full year after the birth of every child. Equal pay for equal work is guaranteed, and job discrimination because of sex is a punishable offense. The pensionable age for women is fifty-five, while it is sixty for men.

The most recent labor code specifically excludes women from some hazardous occupations, and work requiring extreme physical exertion. It also forbids night and overtime work for all pregnant women, and provides for their transfer to lighter work during pregnancies, without any loss in pay. While these regulations lower the average earning power of women, Soviet philosophy holds the interests of society as a whole above that of its individual members, and the protection of women's health is a particular preoccupation of the state interested in raising a steadily declining birthrate.

While winning a complete economic independence from men on the basic level, Soviet woman has not as yet achieved income equality with men in purely monetary terms: it has been estimated that 65 percent of the gross individual earned income is still earned by men. However in view of guaranteed employment and lifelong economic security, inequality in purely monetary terms plays a lesser role than in free-enterprise economies.

Presumably income disparity will disappear in a future communist society where the principle of "to each according to his needs, from each according to his abilities" can be established. The present Soviet formula is "to each according to his work," and thus, disparity of incomes.

4. Politics.

It has been often said that the Soviet state is still run and governed by men. This is partially true. Women's participation in the ruling Communist party and in the administrative councils (soviets) on all levels has never risen over thirty-five percent in head-count terms. Though this is substantially higher than women's participation in government activities of the democratic societies of the world, it still leaves Soviet women seemingly less interested in politics than the man.

The explanation of this situation is that political activity in the Soviet Union, while very time-consuming, is not professional and is unpaid for. It represents the additional *nagruzka* ("loading") on top of a person's usual occupation. Mere membership in the Communist party requires a time investment of several hours each week.

If one calculates the time required for childbirth, child care, and running the household, an average Soviet woman has considerably less spare time than man—simply little free time to give to politics. And many women are perfectly happy to leave politics to the men while devoting their spare time to their homes and families. It is surprising that thirty-five percent of the women find some time to engage in political activity.

In the sphere of politics Soviet woman also started from zero. Before the Revolution, women did not participate in any political or government activity. Her achievement has been great; but because of the many calls for her time it is unlikely her participation in political activities will increase in the foreseeable future.

5. Marriage and Family.

All Tsarist laws applicable to marriage and family— based on the patriarchal church concepts of man being divinely appointed to head and rule his family—were summarily abolished after the Revolution, and replaced by a civil code based on complete equality of the spouses. It was heralded as the most liberal such code in the world.

However conditions prevailing in the country led to flagrant abuses. The code has been modified several times since with the aim of producing the ideal marital union, but preserving a certain legal order. The general trend was to establish the responsibilities of the spouses towards each other and their children besides giving them some very liberal rights.

What are the rights and responsibilities in marriage of Soviet woman, according to the latest revised code?

A woman has the right of free marital choice. She retains her legal identity and her maiden name, if she so desires, and sole property rights to the personal property which she has at the time of the marriage, and to inheritance and gifts she might receive after the marriage. She has the right to engage in any work, even if it prevents marital cohabitation. She has the sole right to regulate her sex activity in marriage since neither of the spouses has any conjugal rights. She has the sole right to terminate any unwanted pregnancy by free medical abortion at any time this is medically permissible. She has the right to terminate her marriage at any time either by mutual agreement with her husband (in absence of underage children), or by a simple court action (required in all cases when underage children are involved). She has the right to contract any number of additional marriages provided that all previous marriages are legally dissolved and all involved underage children's interests are adequately protected.

But she has equal responsibility with her husband to contribute to the economic welfare of the family, and to the children's welfare and education. Both spouses have the equal responsibility to support each other in the case of one becoming sick and disabled. All personal property acquired during the marriage is considered to be common property to be equally divided in the case of divorce.

Women enjoy some special privileges under the code. No husband can obtain divorce for one year after the birth of any child. Women get preferential treatment regarding custody of children and the spouse not living with them pays support for the children.

Theoretically, the ideal Soviet marriage is a free love union of man and woman, economically independent from each other, with the absolutely equal rights and equal responsibilities towards each other, and their children, based on mutual love and respect of all members of the family without any material considerations involved.

Another provision setting Soviet marriage apart from all others is the legal obligation of both partners to bring up their children "in the spirit of devotion to the Motherland . . . and a communist attitude towards work to prepare them for active participation in the construction of communist society."

Compared to the brutally oppressive provisions of the old traditional church marriage in Russia which denied women all legal and property rights, the present Soviet marriage is a vast improvement. It by no means condones marital irresponsibility, and it treats both partners of a marriage with equal severity—in fact it treats women more leniently in some areas.

6. *Sex.*

In matters of sex, men and women are treated absolutely equally by law, more and more so in fact. There are no restrictive laws applicable to women which are not applicable to men. All sex activity is considered to be a private matter as long as it does not outrage public decency. No sex practice is illegal as long as it conforms to the above norms, and moral taboos based on former religious traditions are not recognized.

However in practice, some traditional limitations are still evident. The general attitude towards sex activities among men and women differ, with woman expected to be more restrained and less demonstrative in her sex exercises.

7. Traditional attitudes.

Attitudes die hard, and traditional ones are not altogether dead in Soviet society. The myth of masculine superiority is still alive—not only among men, but women as well. It is still evident in such areas as employment: men are often presumed better suited to assume responsibility than women, even though law forbids any such discrimination.

What can be concluded from this brief excursion into the complex sphere of women's liberation and emancipation during a half century of legal and practical application in a once very backward patriarchal society?

First of all, that given full rights and responsibilities of active citizenship, a woman is capable of competing with men on equal terms in all spheres of creative economic activity. In addition, while fully participating in economic life of her society on all levels, she is also capable of fulfilling her biological functions of life-giver—a human being responsible for the production of the most vital commodity of all: people. Given proper assistance by the society, her motherhood does not interfere with her capacity of being a fully productive and responsible member of this society.

Soviet woman has shown that she is able to live up to her country's expectations of her. But it isn't easy. The average, and especially the above average, Soviet woman is caught in a triple squeeze trying to be a professional woman, prolific mother, and a good housekeeper.

To show how this works in practice, this book closes with some greatly shortened excerpts from a novella by Natalia Baranovskaya entitled "A Week Like Any Other." The story first appeared in *Novyi Mir* (*New World*), the popular literary magazine which courageously published A. Solzenitsin's *One Day in the Life of Ivan Denisovich*.

The heroine of the story, Olga Voronkova, is a young engineer working at an experimental institute. Her husband is also an engineer; they have two children.

A Week Like Any Other

Monday. I'm running, running, and on the stairway I run into Yakov Petrovich. He asks me to come in. I am late—fifteen minutes. Last Monday I was late twelve.

Yakov Petrovich's small eyes are floating in the pink mass of his face . . . He speaks softly and evenly:

"Taking into consideration your interest in our work, and-er-your qualifications, we gave you the position vacated by a junior science collaborator. I won't conceal from you that your-er-lack of punctuality is disturbing us . . ."

I am silent. I love my work. I work conscientiously. But I am often late, particularly on Mondays. I mumble something about the icy sidewalks around our still unfinished apartment block, about buses filled to capacity, about traffic jams . . . and with a sickening feeling I realize that I have said all this before. In an unnaturally hoarse voice I say I'm sorry, and I walk out into the hall . . . I run, and near the lab door remember that I haven't combed my hair this morning. I run to the washroom. I pile pins on the basin rim, comb my hair, look at myself in the mirror, and I hate myself. My unruly hair, my sleepy eyes, my boyish face with large nose and eyes.

I comb my hair, pull down my sweater, then walk slowly along the corridor, trying to organize my thoughts . . . When Yakov Petrovich took me into his group six months ago and assigned me to test new materials, he was

taking a risk. With Lydia Chiastikova who wanted this job
he would have been on safer ground. But this was closer
to my particular speciality, and my knowledge of English
helped. But what if he should ask Lydia to take over now—
after all the tests which I have conducted? Why am I always in a rush, and always late?

The laboratory is our bottleneck. Some installations
have long queues waiting for them. I beg Valentina, the
lab manager, to squeeze me in. She shakes her head nega-
tively, and I beg again. Finally she tells me to try later in
the week.

Now to our test department. There are nine women
working in our room, even though there are only seven
desks. But some girls are always away, working in factories. Today I have a desk for myself—and I have wasted
forty minutes of this desk time!

When I enter, six pairs of eyes meet me. I explain
that I am late because I stopped at the lab. Ludmilla's eyes
show her alarm. Lucia's burning Armenian eyes are full
of reproach. Maria Matveyevna looks over her glasses.
Alla's heavily made-up eyes are indifferent. Shura's round
eyes become even rounder. And Zenaida's sharp pupils are
condemning me: "The lab indeed! Late again!"

Our own group is composed of Lucia, Ludmilla, and
myself. Yakov Petrovich is our leader. The mainstay is
Lucia Markarian. It was Lucia who was the real author of
the new plastic. But Yakov got the credit for it. I asked
Lucia once, and she just shrugged. "It's a funny story." I
have never asked again.

I take my place. And suddenly I see a long questionnaire on the desk with my name on it. "A Questionnaire
for Women." I glance through it. Composition of your
family . . . number of children . . . ages . . . Relatives living with you . . . That's easy: one husband, two
children; no grandparents to take care of them. Where

are your children when you are at work? Mine are in a crèche and in a kindergarten. Housing conditions? Well, I have the best. A new apartment, three rooms, all conveniences. They want to know everything. How many hours during an average week do you spend (a) doing housework, (b) taking care of the children, (c) cultural activities and sports?

Well, my favorite sport is racing. From home to bus, from bus to metro, bus again. Metro again. To work and back. Shopping. I'm a qualified long distance runner.

My humor wilts when I see the next question. Days missed from work because of your or your children's illness? My sore spot. Our bosses know that I have two small children; but have they counted all the days I have missed because of them? It is December now . . . In November both children had the flu. Two weeks I think. In October—colds. I think five days. In September, the chicken pox. With the quarantine, almost three weeks . . . And what about the future? Whooping cough, measles and colds . . . colds! Doctors are in a hurry. So are we. We take the kids back to school before they are completely well, and they are coughing and sneezing until spring.

Lucia, Ludmilla, and I step into the corridor. Lucia lights a cigarette. Ludmilla explains: "This morning they came in . . . Demographers. They said they were conducting polls of all women's institutes. What do they want to know?"

Lucia: "Who the hell knows? Statistics is in vogue now. Generally they want to know why women don't want to bear children; and Ludmilla and I have just one apiece. It is all right for you, Ludmilla—you're a single mother. And Olga has fulfilled her quota. But what if they order me to fulfil the plan? Then—goodbye dissertation!"

I look at Ludmilla. Small, plump, curly like a lamb. She has no husband. The father of her Vova failed to men-

tion that he was already married. He just disappeared.
Ludmilla's mother came from the village, thrashed her,
wanted to complain to the authorities. Then wept, cursing
all men, and is now taking care of the boy.

Lucia's husband is a prominent scientist. They have
a large co-op apartment, enough money. Bliss? Wait. Her
husband wants Lucia to quit work and bear more children.
He wants a *normal* family.

We know less about the fourth mother in our room,
Shura. Her husband drinks. She doesn't complain, but we
know it. So it appears I'm the luckiest of all.

Ludmilla takes the joke about the plan seriously.
"What plan? Is there really a plan?" Then, optimistically,
"No, girls! They want to give us mothers some extra bene-
fits. May be a shorter working week!"

Lucia shakes her head: "All they want is more children . . . Look, girls, I have a solution. Why don't we
make a triple exchange? Olga comes to live in my place, I
go to Ludmilla's, and Ludmilla to Olga's."

This time Ludmilla understands that this is a joke.
"You want to change your three-room place for my one
room in a communal house?"

"No, but I'm forced by circumstances. I need a permanent baby-sitter—your mother, and no husband to get
me pregnant. Olga needs a place close to her work so she
won't be always late. Don't worry, Lamb—Olga's Dima is
a darling. And my Suren will be in ecstasy: Olga is younger
and fatter than I."

Maria Matveyevna joins us. "Why this meeting, Comrades?" We all respect her. We admire her idealism. Her
biography is exceptional: communal work in the thirties,
fine war record. Her daughters were raised in children's
homes, they are married, have their own families. She lives
alone, only for her work, professional and political. She is
nearing seventy. We deeply respect Em-Em, as we call her.

I speak sincerely. "We've been discussing children . . . You see I'm twenty-six, have been married for five years, and I have two children . . ."

"It's like a pre-Revolutionary peasant routine," Lucia cuts in. Maria Matveyevna becomes stern. "Don't say that! Olga must be proud to be a good mother and a good worker. She's a real Soviet woman." And I think: Am I really a good mother? And what does being a real Soviet woman mean?

We return to the office. We have time—they won't collect the questionnaires until next Monday. I begin to work. We have done well. We have improved the chemical cohesiveness of our plastic. Now we must start the tests again . . . The more I work on our plastic, the more I become involved. I become completely lost in my graphs. Suddenly I hear a voice over my shoulder:

"It's ten to two, Olga. I'm leaving. What do you want?"

This is Shura. Today it is her turn to do the shopping for all four mothers in our room. We asked to have our lunch break between two and three; the shops are less crowded then. I order some butter, a kilo of veal sausage, some bread. I want to eat here and catch up on the time I have lost. Lucia also stays. She is hungry as a wolf. When Shura returns, we eat up half of my sausage, tearing the bread with our fingers, and washing it down with water from the faucet.

I go back to work. The second part of the day passes quickly. It is leaving time. Again a bus, and again it is crowded. Again a metro. Jammed. The whirlpool of humanity at the Belorusskaya transfer station. I must hurry, hurry, hurry! Dima and the kids will be at home by seven. Another train. I travel in comfort: standing in a corner, leaning against a wall. I'm yawning so much that a young man can't contain himself: "I'd like to know what you were doing last night?" "Nursing my children," I snap, to get rid of him.

I think about this morning. A typical Monday morning. At a quarter to six the alarm clock rings . . . Then I feel Dima's big hand on my back, he is lifting me up:

"Come on, Olga, get up! You'll be rushing like mad again."

I get up and dress. One hook on my belt is missing. No time. I run into the kitchen, stumble over the rug in the hall. I strike a match and burn my fingers: I forgot to turn on the gas. Finally, the bathroom. I wash, bury my face in a soft towel as if falling asleep for a split second. Then I wake up, muttering, "Hell, what a life!"

Nonsense, Olga! Life is good. You have an apartment in a new house. Kostia and Gulika are fine kids. You have an interesting job. Dima and you love each other. Wonderful.

Tuesday. I get up normally. At ten past six I am ready, except my hair. I peel potatoes for supper, stir the porridge, warm coffee and milk, wake up Dima, and go to get the kids up. I switch on the light in their room. Good morning, my darlings! I snatch Gulika out of her crib. She screams. I call Dima; but he is shaving. A new sound from the kitchen: I forgot to turn off the gas under the milk. I drop Gulika and run.

I'm trying to get the kids up. Dima is setting the table, but can't find something, so he calls me. Meanwhile Gulika hides my comb somewhere. No time to look for it. Finally we are at the table. The kids drink milk and eat rolls. Dima eats. I gulp down some coffee.

Ten to seven. Dima is still eating. I must dress the kids. I work like a demon: warm stockings, warm pants, sweaters, mittens. Kostia struggles. Finally Dima joins me.

The kids are ready. I pull on my boots and find the comb in one of them.

I turn the kids over to Dima, run down the hill towards the bus. A long line. Buses come crowded, take only two or three people on, and leave. At the last moment I rush on, grab the door rail and hang on. Someone pulls me in.

I reach the institute on time. First to Valentina about the tests. "I told you—the *second part* of the week!" I get to my office. Begin to work. Then, to the library to get some American magazines. Only here do I notice that it is five to two. And I haven't placed my shopping order yet.

I find a real meeting going on in the office. All the women from our floor are there. Discussing the questionnaire.

"Ask Olga!" somebody cries.

Em-Em explains: "Zenaida has raised a question: must a woman—Soviet woman—take into consideration the state interests in planning her family?"

I am an authority: two children in less than four years. They have been discussing the questionnaire: If you have no children, indicate the reasons: medical, housing conditions, family status, personal considerations, etc.

Alla thinks the question is monstrous tactlessness. Ludmilla defends it: "We must find a solution for the demographic crisis!" Lydia who has two steady admirers, but no husband, cuts in: "Let those who are married find the solution." Varvara Petrovna corrects her: "This is a national problem and it involves all women—up to a certain age." (She is past it.) Lucia shrugs, "Why waste time discussing such a senseless question?"

Em-Em doesn't like this. "We have done a colossal job in freeing our women, and they should cooperate to help the state, if necessary!"

"May be there should be a practical approach," Lucia says. "In France they pay a premium for each child—"

"Just like on a pig farm?" Alla asks sharply. "Children are not pigs!" Em-Em reproaches her. "Besides, France is a capitalist country."

I am tired of this, and I'm hungry. It is time for one of us mothers to go shopping. Then I must comb my hair. I strike a pose. Everyone turns towards me.

"Comrades!" I say. "As a mother of a multiple family, I can assure you that I have produced children solely guided by national interests. And I challenge you all to a productivity competition."

My joke provokes a virtual riot. All speak at the same time. "She makes a circus out of a serious problem!" "If one is moved by animal instincts—!" "Childless women are egotists!" "Spoiling their own lives!" "We must voluntarily raise the birth-rate!" "Who will pay our pensions if there aren't enough workers?" "Only a woman bearing children is a real woman!" And then Em-Em's angry basso: "Why such noise, Comrades? It is up to everyone to choose her own fate!"

And then Zinaida's little egotistical soul comes to the surface: "Yes, but we have to work for them while they are having their kids."

On my way home I think about it all. Did I choose my fate? I remember how Gulika was born. We didn't want another child. Kostia was just one and a half, when I discovered I was pregnant. I put my name on the abortion list. But then some women told me that judging by my size this time I would have a girl. I left the clinic and came home. "I want to have a daughter," I told Dima. We quarreled. But then Dima relented. "All right, stop crying! You win—we'll have another child. But what if it is another boy?"

It was a girl. I quit my job at the factory. Dima took on some extra work. We started to economize. I reproached Dima for his cigarettes. I could not cope with two children and we sent Kostia to a boarding crèche.

Did I choose all this? No. Am I sorry? No, a hundred times, no. I love my children.

I am running home. The shopping bags hit my knees. I run across the icy empty lot, up the stairway. Of course —the kids are chewing. Dima has given them some bread! I light all the burners—potatoes, milk, tea. Throw some meat balls in the frying pan. In twenty minutes we are eating.

After the meal the kids are sleepy. Quickly—a shower and to bed. By nine they are asleep. Heaven.

Dima has his tea, reads the newspapers. I clear the table, wash the dishes, wash the children's things (they are always filthy), prepare their clothing for the morning. Dima brings in his overcoat—a button has been torn off in the metro. I sweep, collect the garbage, and Dima takes it out.

Everything is finished, and I take my shower. Meanwhile Dima makes our bed. Already in bed I remember that I haven't sewed the hook on my belt. But now no force in the world can get me from under the blankets. I feel Dima getting into bed, but I'm too tired to open my eyes, or return his kiss.

Wednesday. Everyone is ashamed about yesterday's discussion, and we work in silence. The electrical lab. Ludmilla is already there—flirting with a new technician. A strange girl. She told me she wanted to be a dressmaker. "But who is marrying dressmakers these days?"

Today it is my day to go shopping. People waiting in line are grumbling. "Are you buying for a restaurant? And we must wait!" It is best not to hear anything. As I load my shopping bags, I hear a remark behind me: "And they all complain they have no money."

Lugging my bags back I pass a hairdressing salon. I still have twenty minutes. Just enough for a quick trim. A young woman with shaved eyebrows ruins my head. I am ready to cry. But then a manager calls in a young man. "Look, Lenya, they cut this girl's hair upstairs. Can you do something with it?"

"I suggest a boyish bob," Lenya says. He works swiftly while I close my eyes. Finally I open them. I look in a mirror and see a funny young girl. I smile at her, she smiles at me. I laugh. Lenya grins. I slip a ruble into his hand and look at my wrist watch. Twenty past three!!

I'm out of breath when I reach our room. Of course! The boss has been asking for me. I run to the library where he is waiting. He looks at me and smiles. "You've become younger . . . I wanted you to help me translate a page."

He gives me an English book. While I translate, I see Ludmilla through a glass door making signs to me. What has happened? I translate—not one page, but three! I'm on pins and needles. Finally I finish, Yakov thanks me, and I run out looking for Ludmilla. She tells me that she has learned *from reliable sources* that the mechanical lab will be fulfilling a rush order. And what about us?

I must pressure Valentina, or we'll get stuck, and to get stuck in December is a disaster. The plan that must be fulfilled, the year's report. I rush everywhere, but I can't find Valentina. Is she hiding?

Fifteen minutes before leaving time Zinaida begins to distribute theater tickets. A new play. This is not for me and Dima. His mother is taking care of his sister's children, and my Aunt Vera lives in Leningrad. No one can relieve us.

I walk out. Fresh snow on the sidewalks. Clean, fresh air. I decide to walk part of the way home, thinking of nothing, just enjoying the walking, and remembering the days when I was a carefree young girl.

Thinking was a bad idea. I'm late! I'm running down the metro escalator, my bag as always hitting my leg . . . At home, the three of them are walking around, bread slices in their hands. In ten minutes I put a puffy omelette on the table.

The kids run into the kitchen. Kostia looks at me and cries, "Daddy, look! Mamma is a boy!"

Dima smiles. During the supper he doesn't read a newspaper, and glances at me now and then. He helps me with the dishes, and even sweeps the floor. "Olga . . . you're just as you were five years ago."

Because of this we forget to set the alarm clock.

Thursday. I jump up at half past seven! Dima runs to get the kids up. I rush into the kitchen. Only milk and coffee. Then to the nursery to help Dima. By a miracle it looks that we have beaten the clock.

Suddenly Kostia begins to cry. "Maya Mikhailovna punishes me for nothing . . ." We begin to dress him, he is struggling. "Kostia! Daddy and I will be late for work!" He is crying his heart out. Finally Dima promises Kostia to speak to the head nurse. I'm almost crying myself. It seems terrible to take him there by force. I beg Dima to speak to that woman, to find out what has happened.

"There are twenty-eight of them there. One can make a mistake," Dima grumbles.

Now Gulika begins to cry. I can't stand it. I push her towards Dima, and I run out. This morning I am storming the buses, and I make the third.

While riding, I think about Kostia. Yes, there are twenty-eight kids in the nursery instead of the regulation twenty-five. When they are opening the nursery, they tried talking me into working there. "Good pay . . . and a nanny to help you." Good heavens! Twenty-five pants, scarves, coats, hats, folding beds, fifty stockings, felt boots, mittens. Dress, undress, feed them, take them for two walks a day. Who has figured out such work norms for two women? Probably someone who had no children, or whose children didn't go to kindergartens.

Only in the metro do I remember: tonight we have a political class, and it is my turn to prepare a theme. Never mind—I'll think up something.

My first problem is the mechanical lab. Once more Valentina is not there. I leave a note for her. Then I come to our room. Still, our girls are nice. Everyone is admiring my new hairdo. Not a word about my being late again. Then they tell me that Valentina wants to see me.

I rush out, but they call me back. Dima is on the telephone. He spoke to the nurse, and everything is fine. Only after hanging up, I remember that I haven't told him about the class tonight, and that I'll be an hour and a half late. And nothing is prepared! To call Dima at his place is almost impossible. Never mind, later, I must see Valentina.

She tells me that they are having a general production meeting tonight, and from four o'clock on all installations will be free. Four! And the class starts at a quarter to five! I try to explain, but she won't listen. "That's your problem. There are other people wanting this time." I promise to be there.

Walking back, I'm thinking. No, no one can replace me at the lab. There is only one solution. I must pretend I have forgotten about the class. Let them reprimand me tomorrow.

At my desk I go to work. Ludmilla is budging me: "What do you want me to buy for you?" I give her a three-ruble bill. Some meat, anything. And something for a snack here. (I haven't eaten breakfast today.)

They call me to the shipping room. Some packages for me. Samples. I ask for Youra, our handy boy, but of course, as usual, he is not there. I lug the packages to the third floor. And here Ludmilla accosts me: "Olga! They have Lotus today! I put our names on the list, but somebody must go and get it."

Lotus is a detergent powder. We need it very much, but today I can't think about it. It's past three, and I have not set up my tests. In the bag on my desk I find two rolls and some cream cheese. But I have no time to eat.

At five to four I sneak out of the room.

In the lab I begin to work. I adjust the power hammer. It falls. Hurray! The plastic holds. Now to do all the other tests—cohesion, density, compression, stress. It is good to work in a deserted lab. Suddenly I hear a voice: "Voronkova! Voronkova!"

Trapped. Lydia is in the doorway. I collect my samples and run out. The class is already on. It is terrible that I haven't warned Dima . . . We have a new political instructor, a retired colonel. It seems to me he looks at me with reproach.

Finally the class is over. I grab my purse and race to the coatroom. A quarter to seven! I'll get a taxi!

Of course, there's no taxi. Bus. Metro. Completely covered with sweat I reach our place. It is almost nine. The kids are already asleep, dressed. Gulika in the crib, Kostia on the divan. In the kitchen, at the table piled high with dirty dishes, sits Dima reading a technical book, and eating a cold eggplant sandwich.

I tell him about the mess of a day which I have had, but he doesn't accept my excuses. I should have called to warn him. I don't try to defend myself. He is right. What did he give the kids? Some milk, bread, cold eggplant, he

says. I want to undress Kostia and take him to bed, but
Dima protests. "Let's eat first." I don't argue. I cover
Kostia up, return to the kitchen and whip up an enormous
dish of eggs and sausages.

We eat. The house is bedlam. Everything is where we
left it this morning. The children's things are piled on the
floor. Dima hasn't touched anything. As a protest about my
delinquency as a mother.

After dinner, Dima softens. Together we undress
Kostia, take him to bed, and straighten out our room. Then
I clean up the kitchen, wash, do some laundry. I go to bed
after midnight. And at half past two Gulika awakens us
with her crying. Colic and diarrhea. Cold milk and egg-
plants! We have to wash her, change her linen, warm water
for a water bag. "She'll be all right in the morning," Dima
tells me.

In the morning, yes. But meanwhile I'm sitting next
to the crib, holding the hotwater bag against Gulika's
stomach and humming, "Hush, baby, hush—a little rabbit
sleeps under a bush . . ." My arm rests on the rim of the
crib, and my head on my arm.

I go back to bed at about four. And just as I close my
eyes—the alarm clock!

Friday. In the morning everyone in the office is after
me for having tried to skip the political class. I listen, and
I think about the children. We took Gulika to the crèche,
even though she should have stayed at home. I could have
missed a day. No! They would precribe analyses and tests.
Several days. So we took her to the crèche.

We go to work. This is the end of the week. Everyone
is busy. We must finish unfinished work, write reports. And
during the lunch break—manicure, hair. And we mothers
must do the shopping—for three days.

And then the questionnaire! We send Ludmilla to the timekeeper's office to get the list of days we have missed. I know I will be the champion.

I start working. I need my general graph and I can't find it. I look and look, getting desperate. Did I take it to the lab yesterday? I run there. It is not there. I have lost the work of several days!

I come back, slump into a chair, numb all over. I can't think any longer. And suddenly I feel Lucia's hand on my shoulder. I press my face to her hand. Tell her that I have lost my graph.

"And what's this?" she says indicating a big folded paper on my desk. I open it. The graph! I begin to laugh, and I can't stop. Lucia grabs my hand, and pulls me into the hall. I keep laughing, tears running down my cheeks.

"Olga, you're a nut!"

"You're a nut yourself . . ." I say softly. I wipe my face with a handkerchief. "I was just laughing. I have a very funny life, a real cocktail . . . No, I'm not a nut, not yet. But look at these shadows under your eyes. You're a real case."

"I've been a case for years. But I'm six years older than you, and you know my home life . . . But you're young, healthy, you have a fine husband . . . You're intelligent, you're full of life, you're—all right! Let's go shopping together and you'll tell me everything!"

Outside I tell her about my work, my trouble with the lab, my boss. About the children.

Lucia listens sympathetically. "Olga, do you remember you asked me once about this new plastic and Yakov Petrovich? Well, it's a funny story. I had the original idea . . . but I was pregnant, and I decided to have a baby. I knew I couldn't finish the work, and so I gave it all to Yakov. Now it's his baby, and I haven't got mine. I got scared at the last moment, and had an abortion. As always, without telling my husband about it. It was simple—a business trip to Leningrad for a few days. I never tell him when I'm pregnant."

I find her hand and squeeze it.

The shops are jammed, but we work like a shock team, and fill four enormous bags. At three o'clock we start back. And suddenly we see Shura running to meet us. "Let me help you!"

We put Shura in the middle, and now carry the bags together. We step off the sidewalk and have to stop now and then to let the cars drive by.

"Hey, girls—do you need some manpower?" two boys yell at us.

"You're too late!" I yell back. "We have some of our own manpower at home!"

I feel fine, happy. Because the day is sunny, because there are three of us. Because I'm not alone.

We return to the office. Ludmilla brings in the list. Of course, I'm in first place! Seventy-eight missed days! I feel ashamed, as if I were guilty of something. Yes, of being a mother of two children. Now, the questionnaire.

We mothers hold a council. Three of us live in suburban developments and spend almost three hours traveling daily. And what about this question: Indicate the time spent each week taking care of the children? What week? This, or any week?

"I'm taking this one," I say. "This is an average week."

How can any woman figure out the time doing things at home? Lucia suggests that we deduct the working time, time spent traveling and sleeping, and proceed from there. We do that, and we're surprised. It appears that we have between forty-eight and fifty-three "free" hours each week! Then why do we always leave so much undone? Who knows? Who knows how much the so-called family life takes out of woman's life?

I decide to take the questionnaire home. So does Lucia. We have a lot to do this afternoon.

The trip home is a disaster. I have two heavy bags, everything except vegetables. The metro is jammed. I stand in the corner, one bag in my hands, another between my legs. I'm trying to figure out how much I have spent. It always seems to me that I have lost some money. The men sitting around me are either reading, or pretending to be half-asleep in order not to give their seats to the standing women.

The transfer station. A mob waiting for buses. I try to get into a full one, slip off the step, hit my knee. Everybody shouts, and I scream. A husky man pulls me in. I almost fall on my bags. Someone offers me a seat. I inspect my torn stocking and bleeding knee. Then the bags. Only a few eggs broken, and one milk carton squashed. I'm terribly sorry about the stocking—my best four-ruble pair.

I stumble home. The children run into the hall. Dima takes the bags from my arms. A crazy woman . . . Kostia jumps at me and almost knocks me down. Gulika demands an orange. I show my knee, hobble into the bathroom. Dima gets out some iodine and cotton. Everyone is sorry for me. I'm a heroine, and I like it.

I like Friday evenings: we can linger at the table, play with the children, and let them stay up longer. I don't have to launder anything. And I can soak in the bathtub.

But tonight, after last night's trouble with Gulika, we are very tired. We put the kids to bed, and leave everything in the kitchen as it is.

I'm in bed. Dima is still in the bathroom. I am very sleepy, but suddenly I become scared that Dima might by mistake set the alarm clock. I push it under the bed. But I still hear it ticking. I carry it to the kitchen, and lock it in the china closet.

Saturday. On Saturdays we sleep late. We would have slept even longer, but the children get up shortly after eight. Saturday morning is the happiest time of the week: two full days of rest ahead.

While Dima busies himself with the children, I clean up the kitchen and prepare a colossal breakfast. Then I send Dima out with the children, and go to work. First of all, I start a soup. While it is cooking, I clean the house. I dust everything, wash the floors, shake the blankets on the balcony. (Which is wrong.) I sort out the laundry. Dima's things and my things go into the Lotus. Sheets and other large things go to the laundry. Now I grind the meat, peel the potatoes, make a fruit compote. We eat around three. It is late for the children, but they must get the maximum of fresh air.

Dima and the kids come back. Kostia asks Dima to read to him, but Gulika is restless. I put her to bed—otherwise we won't have any peace. I rock her to sleep (which is wrong), and put her into the crib.

Now I must straighten the kitchen again, wash the dishes, clean the stove, mop the floor. Then wash my hair, launder other things, iron the kids' clothes, mend Gulika's tights, and sew the missing hook on my belt.

Dima takes the things to the laundry. Kostia insists on going too. They take the toboggan, and leave. Now I'm alone and can really work. By seven the *men* return and want some tea. Here I remember that Gulika is still asleep. I get her up and she starts to bawl. I pass her to Dima, and start preparing supper. I want them to eat earlier because I must bathe the children. Gulika fusses—she has slept too long.

I bathe Kostia first. But Gulika also wants to get into the tub. "Dima! Take your daughter!" I shout.

"I must work tonight. I'm sorry."

I carry Kostia to his bed. Usually Dima does this, but he is buried in his technical books. Passing him I say: "Incidentally, I also have a higher education."

"Congratulations," he says, sourly.

This strikes me as terribly cruel. I am bathing Gulika and I see my tears dropping into the water. Gulika babbles and tries to get out of the tub. I smack her behind, and she begins to scream. Dima barges in, says angrily, "Don't take it out on the kids!"

"Aren't you ashamed of yourself?" I cry. "Can't you see how tired I am?"

Now I'm crying loudly, muttering that the more I do, the more remains undone, that my youth is going, and that I haven't sat down once since the morning.

Suddenly there is Kostia's scream from the nursery, "Daddy! Don't beat Mamma—don't beat Mamma!"

Dima grabs Gulika, and runs to the nursery. I follow him. Kostia stands up in his bed covered with tears. I take him into my arms, try to calm him down. Dima and I stand close together, the kids in our arms.

"Mamma is just tired . . ." Dima says. "Her arms hurt . . . her legs . . . her back . . . Poor, poor Mamma . . ."

That is all I need. I push Kostia into his arms, run to the bathroom, grab a towel, put it to my face, and begin to sob so bitterly that my whole body is shaking. Dima comes in, embraces me: "Enough . . . Calm down . . . Forgive me . . ."

Now I am already ashamed. What has come over me, anyway?

Dima doesn't allow me to do anything any more. He

puts me to bed, like a child, and brings in some tea. I drink it, and he tucks me in. I fall asleep listening to his footsteps, the sound of running water, the clattering of dishes.

I wake up, and I don't know what time it is, what day. The room is almost dark. The lamp on the table is covered with a newspaper. Dima is reading. I see part of his forehead, his cheek. It looks hollow, he looks tired. "Poor Dima . . . His life isn't easy either . . . And then, my hysterics . . . Dima, I love you . . ."

He gets up, looks at me and smiles: "Still alive, darling?"

I pull my arms from under the blanket, and reach for him.

Sunday. We are lying in bed, just lying, my head touching his chin, his arm around me. We talk about all sorts of small things, the vegetables that must be bought today, about Kostia and his kindergarten.

"Dima, do you think our love can last forever?"

"Well, we ourselves don't last forever."

"That's understood . . . But what is love, in your opinion?"

"Well . . . when people feel comfortable with each other, like you and me."

"And when they produce children?"

"That too . . . That's a part of life . . . Well, we'd better get up now . . ."

"And even when they have no time to talk to each other?"

"Well, what do you want to talk about?"

I am silent. I don't know what I want to talk about. I just wanted to talk. Not about the vegetables, but I can't find a topic.

"We have the last five-ruble bill in the box," I say.

Dima laughs. Some conversation!

I am irked. "Why do you laugh? We can only talk about money, food, and, well, the children."

"Don't be silly. We talk about many things."

"What things. Tell me."

Dima thinks. And I think, Aha, I've caught you!

"Well, about politics . . ." he says. "About the cosmos—many times . . . About figure skating—is it sport or art. About Vietnam, Czechoslovakia . . . About a new TV set and the fourth channel . . . Incidentally, when are we going to get a color TV set?"

"We have five rubles in the box."

"We have our fund!"

Yes, we have a special fund for purchases. It is kept in my old purse. We need many things. A raincoat for Dima, shoes for me, a new dress (this is a must), summer things for the kids. And the fund is growing very slowly.

"You're spending too much on food," says Dima.

"It's because you eat too much," I say.

Dima is offended. So am I. We are now sitting in bed, facing each other. One word leads to another. Finally Dima says: "If you're incapable of coping with the household finances, just say so!"

I jump out of bed. "Yes, I'm incapable of doing anything! I'm stupid."

I run into the bathroom, throw some cold water on my face. "Enough," I tell myself. Finally I get hold of myself. Why am I so irritable? I don't know. Perhaps because I'm always afraid of becoming pregnant, because I'm taking those pills. And do I need this kind of love at all? I am sorry for myself, sorry for Dima. A warm shower calms me. I come out refreshed and more gentle.

The kids are laughing and screaming, playing with Dima. I get out some clean things and we dress them.

During breakfast we plan the day. We must get the

vegetables, I must wash the children's things, and iron everything.

"Aw, forget it!" Dima says. "Let's go out. Look, what a wonderful sunny day."

I surrender. I can do all these things after lunch. We take the toboggan and go to the canal. The children frolic and scream, and we horseplay and laugh.

We return cold, hungry and happy. I decide to feed Dima first, and then send him out for the vegetables. I cook macaroni, warm up the soup and cutlets. After my outing I am a new woman, full of life. Having eaten, I put the children to bed and send Dima out. Now I attack everything at once: throw the laundry into the tub, cover the table with a blanket and get out the iron. And suddenly I decide to shorten my skirt. Why walk around like an old woman, with my knees hidden? I cut away the extra material. That is how Dima finds me when he comes back. I arrange my new skirt around myself and Dima looks at it with sceptical condescension.

"It will be twenty below tomorrow, and you'll be sorry. However, I admit that you have beautiful legs."

I begin to iron the pleats. Dima asks me to iron his pants while I'm at it. I protest. While working I tell him about the questionnaire, and all the days I have missed from work.

"Look, Olga," he says. "May be it's best for you to stop working for a while?"

"And you want me to stay at home all the time? And how are we going to live on what you're earning?"

Dima makes a sweeping gesture. "Well, if I'm free from all *this,* I can do much better. I can bring in two hundred—two hundred and twenty a month. If we deduct all the unpaid time you take off work, it would amount to the same thing. It's a matter of simple economics."

I protest: "So I get all the drudgery, and you get all

that's interesting! A matter of economics! Such a capitalist!"

Dima grins. "This is not a matter of money. It would
be better for the children . . ."

"Dima," I say firmly. "You know I'd do anything for
the kids. But what you suggest would destroy me. Five
years of university, my diploma, my seniority, my dissertation. All that out of the window? And what sort of woman
would I be sitting at home? Always angry, irritable, nag-
ging. No, no, and no!"

"Sorry, Olga. You are probably right. I thought that
perhaps we could arrange our life—well, more efficiently.
Well, I'm sorry I have mentioned it."

Dima walks out. I am sorry for him. Then I hear his
voice from the nursery. Dima is getting the kids up. They
drink milk. Shall we go for another walk? We decide
against it. Dima has had enough, and it would ruin my
evening. And I have so much to do.

Kostia sits on the floor, playing with his building
blocks. Gulika interferes. Kostia cries. So does Gulika.
Then I make a "daughter" for her. It is her own old pa-
jamas stuffed with rags. I attach an old small pillow to it,
and draw eyes and a mouth on it. Gulika does not like
dolls, but she loves the "daughter," carries her around,
speaks to her.

Sunday evening goes on peacefully. The kids play,
Dima works, I iron and prepare supper. I must not forget
that hook on my belt, I tell myself. Finally, all is done.
Now, the questionnaire! After the kids go to sleep.

When they are asleep, after their usual fussing, we
collect the building blocks, and I finish the ironing and the
dishes. I still have some time. To read something, or watch
the TV? Hell, the questionnaire! I sit down to work on it.
Dima looks over my shoulder, passes remarks. I tell him
not to bother me, and finally I finish it. This takes prac-

tically all my *free* time of the week, but they can't complain. Two children—and I'm still young!

Now to get a book and curl up on the divan.

"Hey, what about my pants?" Dima remembers.

We strike a bargain. I will iron his pants, and he will read aloud to me. But he doesn't want any fiction—such waste of time? So we settle on the new issue of *Science Magazine*. He reads about some surgery technique, but I can't follow it without looking at the diagrams. Finally Dima goes to our room, leaving me with my ironing.

I am in bed. Dima brings out the alarm clock, winds it up and sets it, and puts out the light. Only then do I remember the hook on my belt. Well, to hell with it!

In the middle of the night I wake up, and I don't know why. I am disturbed. I get out of bed carefully, trying not to wake up Dima, and walk to the nursery. The children are asleep. I cover them up, feel their foreheads. They seem to be cold. The children sigh, mutter something in their sleep. Quietly, cozily.

What is disturbing me? I don't know. I lie in bed with open eyes, listening to the night's silence. The radiators bubble, there are footsteps in the apartment upstairs. And the alarm clock is ticking away—unceasingly, mercilessly.

So one more week has gone by. A week like any other.

Socialism has solved many things for our Soviet sisters, but it has not removed the Biblical curse placed on woman in the Garden of Eden. Or was it a blessing? But the point remains: Soviet woman is little different from all other women in the world with love forever playing the paramount part in their existence. And one can only hope that nothing will ever make them surrender this priceless gift bestowed on them by nature for in that lies their enormous strength—and, conversely, the best hope for mankind's survival.